MASSAGE NATIONAL EXAM

QUESTIONS AND ANSWERS

Daphna R. Moore, CMT, LMT, NA

Retired AMTA Massage Instructor

Hughes Henshaw Publications • Palm Bay, FL 32907

Library of Congress in Catalog Publication Data

Moore, Daphna LMT, CMT, NA, Retired Member of AMTA Massage Instructor

Massage National Exam Questions and Answers

New Revised Edition – 2008

ISBN 1-892693-36-4

Thirteenth Edition February 2008

INTERNATIONAL STANDARD BOOK NUMBER
1-892693-36-4
Published in the United States of America
By

HUGHES HENSHAW PUBLICATIONS
424 Hurst Road NE
Palm Bay, FL 32907

www.massagenationalexam.com
hugheshenshaw@aol.com

321.956.8885 ● 321.956.2475

1. Name three of the dense connective tissues.
   Tendons, ligaments, and joint capsules.

2. What is the name of the spongy layer just below the skin?
   Superficial Fascia

3. How do you differentiate superficial fascia from muscles?
   Pick up the skin and the superficial fascia, and then contract the underlying muscles.

4. What is Orthopedic Massage?
   Techniques for understanding, assessing, and treating musculoskeletal pain and injury.

5. What is found directly under superficial fascia and what does it cover?
   Deep Fascia. It covers all the muscles and bones blending into ligaments and joint capsules and wrapping organs.

6. Most cases of muscle spasms are actually the result of _____.
   An injury of some other tissue.

7. True or False. Muscles are a major source of pain and injury. **False**

8. True or False. Chronic pain results when an injury heals improperly. **True**

9. What is secreted by the ovaries? **Estrogen**

10. Where does the conception vessel start? **Peritoneum**

11. What is responsible for the cardiovascular blood flow?
    Lymphatic System

12. Ki 1 is found where on the body? **Sole of the foot**

13. Would you perform massage if the client has Thrombophlebitis? **No**

14. Is the Meisner Corpuscle sensitive to touch? **Yes**

15. What gland is associated with the third eye chakra? **Pineal**

16. What would be out of balance in the wood element? **Sight**

17. Why shouldn't you lie on your massage brochures?
    a. it could be misleading
    b. **you want to build trust - correct**
    c. you don't want them to call the authorities

18. What is **extreme** inflammation of the joints? **Rheumatoid Arthritis**

19. When a client tells you they have an eating disorder should you?
    a. inform their doctor
    b. **keep it confidential**
    c. tell husband
    d. do nothing

20. St 36 is on what part of the body? **Anterior Calf**

21. In the 5-element theory what spreads pain to other areas? (Research the answer)
    a. **wind**
    b. dry
    c. moist
    d. heat

22. Where would you place a pillow if a client has back and hip pain? (Research the answer)
    a. head only
    b. head and between legs
    c. head between legs
    d. in front of abdomen
    e. none of the above

23. Energy fields in Aryvedic medicine are _____? **Doshas**

24. The most frequently moveable joint in the body is _____?
    Glenhumeral

25. What movement is most commonly the cause of a lateral side ankle sprain? (Research for the answer)
    a. eversion

      b.   inversion

      c.   pronation

      d.   circumduction

26.   What sense organ is associated with water? **Ears**

27.   What is the most water repellent?

      a.   blood

      b.   skin

      c.   there were other things listed

28.   What is connected to the hypothalamus? **Pituitary Gland**

29.   True or False. In many cases pain is *referred* from the source of energy to another part of the body. **True**

30.   What does the spleen nourish? **Lungs**

31.   What are the three functions of the blood?

Nourish the body, moisten the body, and aid the mind

32.   In Chinese Traditional Medicine Qi has four directions. What are the four?

Ascending, descending, entering and leaving

33.   A woman who had chemo for breast cancer 8 years ago could still have what symptoms?

      a.   Acid reflux

      b.   **Dark areola – It is the dark colored skin that surrounds the nipple.** correct answer

34.   What does histamine do?

It contributes to an inflammatory response, and it causes constriction of smooth muscle.

35.   What is holistic health?

Medical care involving the treatment of the whole person: body/mind/ spirit

36.   True or False. The shoulders, neck, thorax, low back, sacrum, buttocks, and hip joints are the only significant sources of referred pain. **True**

37.   If a client has PTSD (Post-Traumatic Stress Disorder) and just found out they had been sexually abused what should you do?

    a.   Deny massage treatment

    b.   Watch for muscle tremor

    c.   **Refer to psychotherapist - correct answer**

38.   When working on the aiis and the leg is flexed what muscle are you working on?   (Research for the answer)

    a.   Rectus femoris

    b.   Sartorius

    c.   liopsoas

    d.   none of the above

39.   What is Flexion-Addiction and what does it promote?

It is prolonged sitting, couch potatoes, sitting at long hours at computer, sleeping in flexed positions that promotes the following: length-tension, m balances resulting in tight\short hip flexors; and neurologically weakened hip extensors.

40.   What protein would the body rather have as use for energy?

    a.   carbohydrate

    b.   **protein (a protein is a protein no matter what name you give it)**

    c.   fat

    d.   sugar

41.   What muscles are shortened due to prolonged flexed sitting and sleeping?

The ilopsoas and rectus femoris muscles

42.   If someone has a seizure what would you do first?

Stay calm and make sure the area is safe so the person will not be injured and stay with the person until the seizure passes

43.   When someone has gout what mineral is lacking?

Calcium

44.   What part of the colon passes through the pelvic outlet?

    a.   ascending

    b.   transverse

    c.   descending

    c.   **sigmoid**

45. How do you stretch pectoralis major?

   Stand at end of wall or in doorway facing perpendicular to wall. Place inside of bent arm on surface of wall. Position bent elbow shoulder height. Turn body away from positioned arm. Hold stretch. Repeat with opposite arm.

46. What taste is associated with spleen?

   Sweet

47. What organ is located posterior to xiphoid process?

   Liver

48. Where are plantar warts located?

   On the soles of the feet

49. If a client is in 3rd trimester, its okay for them to be in _____ position?

   a. prone

   b. on their back

   c. **supine**

50. If a client has constipation what would you massage first?

   a. **abdomen**

   b. SI

   c. Li

51. True or False.   Pain caused by active movements gives a good indication of what structure is injured.   **False**

52. When the thumb performs circumduction what would you massage first?

   (Research for the correct answer)

53. What is Somatic Resonance?   **Therapist being grounded in their bodily awareness and experience.**

54. By shortening the rectus femoria what exercise will it perform?

   (Research for the correct answer)

55. When you are performing ROM and come across resistance what do you do?

   Stop

56. What tissue covers all organs?
    a. connective tissue
    b. **epithelial   correct answer**
    c. lining

57. If you are giving resuscitation when would you stop?
    a. when professional help arrives
    b. when breathing returns
    c. when you are too tired to continue
    d. **any of the above**

58. Kidney is associated with what chakra?
    6th chakra

59. The 3rd chakra is associated with what pair?
    Solar Plexus/Navel   Action and Will

60. Visceral is part of what system?
    autonomic system which is part of the parasympathetic system

61. Where does the heart meridian begin?
    Under the arm

62. Where does the heart meridian end?
    At the little finger

63. Where do you find the sciatic notch?
    a. L1 S5
    b. L2 S4
    c. L4 S2
    d. **L5 S1**

64. What are ethics?
    Motivations based on ideas of right and wrong

65. Which are associated with the bladder?
    a. **urine storage and output**
    b. the emotion fear and anger

66. Study the elements below. It pertains to the five element theory and organs associated with the elements. Several questions are given on the National Exam pertaining to the oriental elements, etc.

Element	Color	Organ/s	Sense Organs	Taste
Water	Black	Kidneys/ Bladder	Ears	Salty
Wood	Blue/Green	Liver/Gall Bladder	Eyes	Sour
Fire	Red	Heart/ Small Intestine	Tongue	Bitter
Earth	Yellow	Spleen/ Stomach	Mouth	Sweet
Metal	White	Lungs/ Large Intestine	Nose/Sinuses	Spicy

67. When flexing the elbow, what muscle is involved?
Brachioradialis

68. Sea water on the earth would be like (_____) in the human?
Blood

69. Where do you find pulmonary semilunar valve?
Between the left ventricle and the aorta

70. What gland is associated with heart chakra?
Thymus gland

71. Parkinson's disease may start with a slight _____.
Tremor

72. What is synergist to periformis?
   a. Pectineus
   b. Adductor longus
   c. **Gluteus maximus**
   d. Other

73. What muscle would you suggest to stretch for someone who has kyphosis?
Pectoralis

74.   What muscle is involved in flexing the forearm?

Biceps brachii

75.   In Oriental Medicine yang channel flows in what direction?

Down

76.   Where is the sperm manufactured?

In the testes; it is matured and stored in the epididymis, which is part of the male reproductive system.

77.   What is the function of the Lung Meridian?

The Lung Meridian governs the respiratory system, skin, perspiration, and energy and body temperature regulation

78.   A client comes into your office and is having pain when trying to put on a shirt or coat. What muscle is causing the problem?

Rhomboids and supraspinatus

79.   What are two muscles that don't tire easily and what are they called?

Rectus Femoris and Periformis - smooth muscles

80.   What is Ischemia?

Decreased blood flow

81.   What is the sense organ associated with the gall bladder and liver?

Eyes

In Chinese medicine emotions are associated with certain organs. Be sure and study the below list as there are questions on each of these.[1]

SPLEEN

Emotions - worry, dwelling or focusing too much on a particular topic, excessive mental work

Spleen Function - Food digestion and nutrient absorption. Helps in the formation of blood and energy. Keeps blood in the blood vessels. Connected with muscles, mouth, and lips. Involved in thinking, studying, and memory.

Symptoms - of Spleen Imbalance - Tired, loss of appetite, mucus discharge, poor digestion, abdominal distension, loose stools or diarrhea. Weak muscles, pale lips. Bruising, excess menstrual blood flow, and other bleeding disorders.

LUNG

Emotions - grief, sadness, detached.

Lung Function - Respiration. Forms energy from air, and helps to distribute it throughout the body. Works with the kidney to regulate water metabolism. Important in the immune system and resistance to viruses and bacteria. Regulates sweat glands and body hair, and provides moisture to the skin.

Symptoms - of Lung Imbalance - Shortness of breath and shallow breathing, sweating, fatigue, cough, frequent cold and flu, allergies, asthma, and other lung conditions. Dry skin. Depression and crying.

LIVER

Emotions - anger, resentment, frustration, irritability, bitterness, "flying off the handle."

Liver Function - Involved in the smooth flow of energy and blood throughout the body. Regulates bile secretion, stores blood, and is connected with the tendons, nails, and eyes.

Symptoms of Liver Imbalance - breast distension, menstrual pain, headache, irritability, inappropriate anger, dizziness, dry, red eyes and other eye conditions, tendonitis.

HEART

Emotions - lack of enthusiasm and vitality, mental restlessness, depression, insomnia, despair.

Heart Function - Regulates the heart and blood vessels. Responsible for even and regular pulse. Influences vitality and spirit. Connected with the tongue, complexion, and arteries.

Symptoms of Heart Imbalance - Insomnia, heart palpitations and irregular heart beat, excessive dreaming, poor long-term memory, psychological disorders.

KIDNEY

Emotions - fearful, weak willpower, insecure, aloof, isolated.

Kidney Function - Key organ for sustaining life. Responsible for reproduction, growth and development, and maturation. Involved with lungs in water metabolism and respiration. Connected with bones, teeth, ears, and head hair.

Symptoms of Kidney Imbalance - Frequent urination, urinary incontinence, night sweats, dry mouth, poor short-term memory, low back pain, ringing in the ears, hearing loss, and other ear conditions. Premature grey hair, hair loss, and osteoporosis.

82. What emotion is associated with kidneys and bladder?

    Fear

83. In Chinese medicine what color is associated with the heart?

    Green and sometimes pink

84. What is excess fluid build-up in the tissues called?   **Edema**

85. If a new client is hesitant about filling out an intake form, what should you do?

    Ask them the questions and write down what they tell you.

86. Which of the following is a Yin Organ?
    a. Stomach
    b. small intestine
    c. **liver**

87. A client wants to give you a hug after a massage session and you don't feel comfortable. What is this an example of?

    Personal Boundaries

88. When a physician writes out a comfort order, what is this usually for?

    A terminally ill patient.

89. What emotion is associated with the wood element?

    Anger

90. The kneecap is another word for the _____?

    Patella

91.   The collar bone is another term for the_____?
       clavicle

92.   The thigh bone is another word for the _____?
       femur

93.   Which of the following is comprised primarily of dense fibrous tissue?
       a.   adipose tissue
       b.   muscles
       c.   **tendons and ligaments**

94.   Voluntary movements of the skeletal muscles are controlled primarily by the
       _____ _____.   **autonomic system**

95.   A client comes to you saying that he/she is depressed and believes massage
       will cure it, what should you do?
       a.   refuse massage
       b.   agree
       c.   **suggest they seek professional help and continue massage session**

96.   When there is fluid build-up in the lungs, what condition is tapoetment good
       for?
       Chronic Bronchitis

97.   What condition is characterized by softening of the bone and is called rickets in
       young children and _____ in adults?
       a.   osteoporosis
       b.   osteomyeritis
       c.   **osteomalacia**

98.   How can you tell the difference between edema and pitting edema?
       If you press a finger firmly into the tissue and it leaves an indentation.

99.   In oriental medicine what meridian runs up the middle of the spine?
       Governing

**SOME OF THE QUESTIONS BELOW WERE GIVEN ON THE NATIONAL EXAM
IN SEPTEMBER AND OCTOBER 2007 AND YOU MAY NEED TO RESEARCH
SOME OF THE ANSWERS. IN RUSHING TO GET THIS NEW EDITION TO YOU,
WE DID NOT HAVE TIME TO CHECK FOR ALL THE CORRECT ANSWERS FOR
SOME OF THESE QUESTIONS. YOU SHOULD ASK YOUR INSTRUCTOR WHAT
THE ANSWERS ARE AS THEY ARE PART OF THE NATIONAL EXAM. YOU MAY**

FIND SOME OF THE ANSWERS IF YOU GO TO GOOGLE.COM AND TYPE IN THE QUESTION. Some of the questions may have (•) instead of a. b. c. etc.

100. When does HIV start to replicate?

Research or ask your instructor for the answer. It was on the exam In October of 2007.

101. If a person is laughing uncontrollably and talking rapidly, what element are they in excess of?

Fire

102. Which meridian should NOT be treated during pregnancy?   **SP6**

103. Massage on an infant should be short in duration and light because:

- Infants need to be fed and changed regularly
- **The nervous systems of infants are not yet developed**
- Perceptions of touch are formed at an early age

104. What emotion is associated with the large intestine?

Grief

105. Where are epinephron and norepinephron secreted from?

Adrenal medulla

106. What is the origin of the gallbladder meridian?

- Base of the occiput
- Outer eye

107. What is bioenergetics?   **Ask your instructor or google.com.**

108. The chakra associated with grounding is: **1st chakra** (root chakra)

- (all choices were numbers, not names)

109. The chakra associated with communication is:

- (all choices were numbers, not names)

110. Energy fields in Ayurvedic medicine are:

- Tsubos – are acupressure points
- **Meridians**
- Chakras- are wheels of energy
- Doshas

CHART FOR YOU TO STUDY

	Sanskrit Name	Location	Color	Central Issue	Orientation to self	Goals	Rights	Identity	Demon	Element	Excessive Traits	Deficient Traits
Root (1)	Muladhara (root/ support)	Base of spine	Red	Survival, Grounding	Self-preservation	Stability, grounding, health, prosperity, trust	To be here, to have	Physical	Fear	Earth	Heaviness, Sluggish monotony, obesity, hoarding, materialism, greed	Frequent fear, lack of discipline, restless, underweight, spacey
Sacral (2)	Svadhisthana (sweetness)	Abdomen, Genitals, lower back, hips	Orange	Sexuality, Emotions, Desire	Self-gratification	Fluidity, pleasure, healthy sexuality, feeling	To feel, to want	Emotional	Guilt	Water	Overly emotional, poor boundaries, sex addiction, obsessive attachments	Frigidity, impotence, rigidity, emotional numbness, fear of pleasure
Solar Plexus (3)	Manipura (lustrous Jewel)	Solar Plexus That area where you feel it in your gut	Yellow	Power, Will	Self-definition	Vitality, spontaneity, strengthof will, purpose, self-esteem	To act	Ego	Shame	Fire	Dominating, blaming, aggressive, scattered, constantly active	Weak will, poor self esteem, passive, sluggish, fearful
Heart (4)	Anahata (unstruck)	Heart	Green with pink swirls	Love, Relationships	Self-acceptance	Balance, compassion, self-acceptance, good relationships	To love and be loved	Social	Grief	Air	Codependency, poor boundaries, possessive, jealous	Shy, lonely, isolated, lack of empathy, bitter, critical
Throat (5)	Visshudha (purification)	Throat	Blue	Communication	Self-expression	Clear communication, creativity, resonance	To speak and be heard	Creative	Lies	Sound	Excessive talking, inability to listen, over-extended, stuttering	Fear of speaking, poor rhythm
3rd eye (6)	Ajna (to perceive)	Brow	Purple	Intuition, imagination	Self-reflection	Psychic perception, accurate interpretation, imagination, clear seeing	To see	Archetypal	Illusion	Light	Headaches, nightmares, hallucinations, delusions, difficulty concentrating	Poor memory, poor vision, can't see patterns, denial
Crown (7)	Sahasrara (thousandfold)	Top of head	WHITE	Awareness	Self-knowledge	Wisdom, knowledge, consciousness	To know	Universal	Attachment	Information	Overly intellectual, spiritual addiction, confusion, dissociation	Learning difficulties, spiritual skepticism, limited beliefs, materialism, apathy

111.   What meridian is out of balance if client has tendonitis?
   - **Liver**

112.   A client visits your office and is injured as a result of negligence. What insurance protects the massage practitioner/therapist?
   - Personal liability
   - General liability
   - Premise liability
   - Small business

113.   In TCM (Traditional Chinese Medicine), the 4 examinations occur:
   - At home during self-help
   - **At the initial interview**
   - At the exit interview
   - During treatment

NOTE: There are four examination methods: Questioning/history taking, inspection, auscultation (listening) & olfaction (smelling), and palpation. The four methods have their unique clinical functions and cannot be replaced by one another. Sometimes, false manifestations of a disease occur which emphasize the importance of integrating all diagnostic methods.

114.   If the client is in the supine position with the hip laterally rotated, what muscle is shortened?
   - Piriformis
   - Gracilis
   - TFL

115.   What muscles(s) are implicated if the shoulder girdle is elevated?
   - Levator scapula and trapezius
   - Deltoid and levator scapula

116.   The nuchal ligament makes what area difficult to palpate?
   - Anterior neck
   - Posterior neck
   - Sacrum
   - Shoulder

117.   What muscle contracts during inspiration?
   - Internal oblique

- External oblique
- **Diaphragm**
- Serratus anterior

118. The quadriceps eccentrically contract while running downhill to:
- Balance the rectus abdominus
- **Resist gravity**

119. The Conception vessel starts:
- Peritoneum
- Navel
- Chest
- **Deep in Lower Abdomen**

120. Client has extreme kyphosis. Which would make her the MOST comfortable:
- Pillows under the ankles
- Pillows under the knees to lengthen the spine
- **Pillows under the head and neck**

121. In lordosis, which muscle is the antagonist?
- Rectus abdominus
- gluteal muscles (reseach this for correct answer)

122. The most freely movable joint in the body is:
- AC joint
- Sternoclavicular
- **Glenohumeral**
- Ilioacetabulum

123. Endocrine glands secrete:
- **Hormones**
- Neurotransmitters
- Progesterons

124. The tubes that carry urine from the kidney to the bladder are called:
- Ureters

125. The inferior attachment of the levator scapula is the:
- Splenius capitus

- **Superior medial border of the scapula**
- Inferior lateral angle of the scapula

126. What attaches muscles to bones?
- Ligaments
- **Tendons**

127. A sprain occurs:
- In the muscle belly
- At the musculotendinous joint
- **In the ligament**

128. What organs are protected by the sternum and vertebral column?
- **Heart**
- Stomach
- Thyroid

129. A female patient comes into your office and complains of aches and light or severe lower abdominal pain. It could be:
- **Dysmennorhea (painful menstrual periods)**
- Cirrhosis if the liver
- Intestinal polyps

130. A 62 year old man comes to your office with pain down his arm, bluish lips, shortness of breath. You should:
- **Call an ambulance (correct answer)**
- Give him a glass of water
- Help him walk it off

131. Which of the following actions does the biceps brachii perform?
- Supination of the forearm at the radioulnar joint
- **Flex the muscle and rotate the forearm**

132. Bile (and two others) are emptied into the small intestine at the:
- Jejunum
- Ileum
- Duodenum
- **Mesentery**

133. Diverticulitis is a disease of the:
- **Large intestine**
- Small intestine
- Stomach

134. A heart attack is also known as _____? **Myocardial infarction**

135. What substance is needed to strengthen bones, provide muscle contracture:
- **Calcium**
- Vitamin D
- Vitamin C

136. What provides structure to the body and organs:
- Fascia
- **Skeleton**
- Muscles

137. What is the body's preferred energy source?
- **Carbohydrates**
- Proteins
- Fats

138. Massage is intended to activate which system?
- Central nervous system
- Peripheral nervous system
- Sympathetic nervous system
- **Parasympathetic nervous system**

139. Varices are associated with what system?
- Circulatory
- **Digestive**
- Nervous
- Respiratory

140. What form of draping covers the genitals while enabling access to the rest of the body?
- **Diaper**
- Top cover
- Full sheet

141.   Most back injuries occur when lifting when:
- The knees are flexed
- The hip is flexed
- The lift is in front
- **The torso is twisted**

142.   Which classification of practitioner is known for performing subluxations?
- Medical doctor
- **Chiropractor**
  NOTE: Chiropractic "subluxation" is not the same as medical subluxation

143.   Static touch is used:
- to isolate the effects of manipulating soft tissue from those of touching the skin

144.   When running, the point at which the body weight is directly over the leg in contact with the ground is:
- Heel strike
- **Mid-stance**

145.   When psychological influences become physical symptoms it is called:
- **Hypochondriac**
- Psychotic
- Somatic

146.   The liver is located in the:
- **Upper right quadrant of the abdomen**
- Lower right quadrant

147.   Two joints that move in a multi-axial plane are:
- Hip and knee
- Knee and shoulder
- Elbow and hip
- **Shoulder and hip**

148.   The heel bone is the:
- **Calcaneus**
- Talus
- Carpal

149. During treatment, a client who starts to breathe more rapidly may be experiencing:
   - **Anxiety**
   - Relaxation

150. A pathway of nerves associated with a specific pattern on the skin is called:
   - Dermatome
   - **Meridian**

151. You come across a scene with an apparently unconscious person. Your first step should be:
   - Clear the throat of any obstructions.
   - Position the person on his back
   - Tilt the head back
   - **Check for responsiveness**

152. Which receptors sense deep touch?
   - **Pacinian corpuscles**
   - Meissner's corpuscles
   - Golgi tendon receptors

153. The muscle action in which the muscle length stays the same is:
   - **Isometric**
   - Isotonic
   - Twitch
   - Tetanic

154. During the client interview, which of the following would indicate disinterest on the part of the practitioner/therapist?
   - Nodding occasionally
   - Leaning forward with hands in lap
   - **Leaning back with arms crossed and legs crossed**
   - Direct eye contact

155. A doctor might recommend massage for a cancer patient to:
   - Reduce the size of the tumor
   - Cure the disease
   - **Provide comfort and stress reduction**

156.   What's the best way to treat bursitis?
- heat pack
- **ice pack**
- passive range of motion
- other

157.   When you laterally rotate the femur, what muscle shortens?
Piriformis

This section has questions from students who took their exams in 2006.
These questions were on the exam and some may not have an answer.

1.   Touch that conveys sexuality is considered _____. **Erotic**

2.   Define pain. **A subjective experience of the person**

3.   A terminal illness is one where care is_____. **Palliative**

4.   What is diagnosis? **Term used for the signs and symptoms reported by the physician.**

5.   How does a physician refer a patient to you?

6.   What do you consider when sending a patient to a physician?

7.   What do you need to send to the physician so he/she knows how the patient is doing? **Progress Notes**

8.   When do you have to worry about a mole?

9.   What muscle do you palpate most laterally on the popliteal fossa with patient contracting quadriceps?
   • biceps femoris
   • rectus femoris
   • none of the above

10.   What movement occurs in the distal radius?
   • radial deviation
   • flexion
   • pronation
   • **ulnar deviation**
   • other

11.   What is the most common respiratory rate per minute in an elderly patient?
   • 30 to 60
   • 40 to 50
   • 80 to 90
   • **10 to 20**
   • other

12. What vessel do you have to be careful of when working the anterior triangle of the neck (an endangerment site)?
    - jugular vein
    - **carotid artery**
    - other

13. What point would you work on for headaches in Oriental modality?
    - **LI 4**
    - LI 10
    - LI 14
    - other

14. What does the pyloric valve divide?
    - stomach from esophagus
    - esophagus from the large intestine
    - **large intestine from small intestine**
    - esophagus from small intestine
    - other

15. Forward head is almost always related to what?
    - kyphosis
    - lordosis
    - scoliosis
    - other and research for the answer on this question

16. If a patient wants to hug the practitioner after the massage and he/she feels uncomfortable about that, to what code of ethics will these be related to?
    - **personal boundaries**
    - scope of practice
    - sexual harassment (misconduct)
    - standards of practice

17. When you have to massage a long extremity what is the best posture position?
    - put body weight toward the patient, using force from waist (answer)
    - switch feet every once in awhile

18. If someone has low back problems what is the safest way for them to bend?
    - flexing knees and straight back
    - extended knees and bending back
    - flexed knees and back

19. What is the best way to treat someone with digestive problems?
    - Effleurage in the abdominal area
    - deep tissue in the abdominal area
    - work some pressure point

20. What is the name of a muscle that moves the joint to the opposite way from primary movement?
    - synergetic
    - **antagonist**
    - other

21. What muscle is close to the carotid artery?
    - **sternocleidomastoid**
    - splenius capitis
    - trapezius
    - scalenes
    - other

THE FOLLOWING QUESTIONS WERE ON THE NATIONAL EXAM SEPTEMBER and OCTOBER 2007

1.   Earth's season is _____? **Late Summer**

2.   What is the body's preferred energy source? **Carbohydrates**

3.   What vitamin has to do with the bones and the teeth? **Calcium**

4.   What massage do you do when someone is sensitive to touch? **Reiki**

5.   The technique that involves pumping is _____. **Compression**

6.   What provides structure to the body and organs. **Skeletal /bones**

7.   To assess a client's ROM you could put them through a series of _____.
     Joint mobilization

8.   Two joints that move in a multi-axial plane are _____. **Shoulder & hip**

9.   The chakras are associated with what type of glands? **Endocrine-sensory**

10. The root chakra is associated with what sense? **Smell**

11. What organ is NOT associated with Yang? **Liver**

12. True or False. Massage can activate the lymphatic system? **True**

13. The hara (the center of gravity) is located where? **Just below the navel**

14. What action does the biceps brachii perform?
     Biceps curl

15. Diverticulitis is a disease of the what? **Large intestine**

16. The largest artery in the body is the _____. **Aorta**

17. The fight or flight response is controlled by the _____. **Adrenal glands**

18. The tubes that carry urine from the kidney to the bladder are _____.
Ureters

19. What are neurotransmitters? **Chemical messengers**

20. What hormone does the pineal gland produce? **Melatonin**

21. The 1099 Tax Form is used to notify the IRS of _____information?
Independent Contractor Wages

22. What is similar to marmas? **Acupuncture points**

23. What is more important in taking a Continuing Education Program?
    a. **learning something new to enhance professional development**
    b. to become certified in order to gain more clients, respect and more money
    c. I like the instructor

24. What is Zero Balancing?
Zero Balancing is a modality that helps relieve physical and mental symptoms; to improve the ability to deal with life stresses; to organize vibratory fields thereby promoting the sense of wholeness and well being.

25. What is Somatic Resonance?
It is where the therapist is grounded in their bodily awareness and experience.

26. What is one of the most challenging skills in massage?
    a. **listening to our hands while we work and the ability to palpate and respond to the individual tissue variances**
    b. scheduling appointments
    c. doing your taxes

27. What is Chi Nei Tsang?
A Chinese system of deep healing of the use of energy to the five major systems in the body which are: vascular, lymphatic, nervous, and acupuncture meridians.

28. Hereditary information is stored in the _____. **Nucleus**

29.   Which connective tissue is strong in all directions?
        Dense, irregular, collagenous connective tissue

30.   What is the most common cartilage in the body? **Hyaline**

31.   Which layer of the skin acts as an energy storehouse? **Hypodermis**

32.   If your finger is bleeding, you know that the cut is at least as deep as the
        _____.   **Dermis**

33.   What is the most lethal form of skin cancer?   **Melanoma**

34.   Where are adipose cells found?   **In the hypodermis**

35.   Which joint is found between the radius and ulna in the antebrachium?
        Syndesmosis

36.   What is the most common type of joint found in the body?   **Synovial**

37.   Fill in the blank by completing the following sequence: abdominal aorta,
        common iliac artery, _____, femoral artery.   **External iliac artery**

38.   A deficiency of dietary iodine results in the development of _____.   **A
        goiter**

39.   Which movement should be avoided for someone with a hip replacement?
        Abduction of the hip

40.   Massage of _____ muscle group would be effective in relieving sciatica?
        Gluteus group

41.   What causes poliomyelitis?   **A viral infection**

42.   The mitral valve is also known as the _____?   **Bicuspid valve**

43.   What are warts?   **A contagious infection of the epidermis layer of the
        skin**

44.   Proper draping is a very important part of professional business ethics. Why is
        this so?
        It ensures your client's privacy and comfort

45. Which muscle attaches to the zygomatic arch? **Masseter**

46. Can massage reduce pain and if so, in what way?
    Yes. It reduces the cause behind pain stimulation.

47. When you roll a bowling ball forward, what is the primary movement of the shoulder? **Flexion**

48. When you stand on your tip-toes your ankle joint goes through_____.
    Plantarflexion

49. What action are the erector spinae muscles capable of? **Extension**

50. What muscle of the transversospinalis group is found primarily on the cervical and upper thoracic spine? **Semispinalis**

51. What type of joint is located between two adjacent vertebrae? **Symphysis**

52. _____ is the layer of dense irregular connective tissue that is around all bones. **Periosteum**

53. True or False. Type I Diabetes Mellitus is characterized by a lack of insulin production by the beta cells within the pancreatic islet cells. **True**

54. True or False. CST (CranioSacral Therapy) works through thecrainosacral system to facilitate the performance of the body's inherent self-corrective mechanisms and thereby normalizes the environment in which the central nervous system functions. **True**

55. How many milligrams of magnesium per day should a massage therapist or anyone else for that matter consume? **400 to 800 milligrams to supplement your diet**

56. What are the three steps in helping your clients with chronic pain?
    Understand the emotional dimension of chronic pain; help your client realize other healing resources i.e. acupuncture, yoga, etc.; and create a safe space so your client feels safe, learn body language, move slowly, respect the boundaries of the client and   don't impose your own ideas of what the session should be like.

57. True or False. On your intake form referencing pain with 0 being no pain and 10 being worse pain, would you, as a therapist, ask about emotional (psychological) pain? **True**

58.   Name the five types of scars.   **Hypertrophic, keloid, trauma, surgical, and burn**

59.   What system is the key to restoring muscle memory?   **Nervous system**

60.   What are the two most common joint problems that massage therapists treat?

Osteoarthritis and rheumatoid arthritis.

61.   What are seven steps in setting up a safe and effective work area?

Create comfort by providing all the necessary toiletries i.e. clean sheets, drinking water, make sure the room temperature is comfortable, have controlled lighting, ensure privacy, have a neat treatment room, have a clock in your room that is silent, make sure all equipment is set up properly and in working condition, make the room secure for yourself, as well as for your client.

True or False on Insurance Billings

62. True or False. A massage therapist can accept any type of insurance case.
False

63. True or False. As a massage therapist I do not have to keep precise records or documentation.
False

64. True or False. It is not illegal for a massage therapist to bill for a medical massage.   **True**

65. True or False. A massage therapist can safely and effectively without insurance billing training, bill insurance companies.   **False**

66. True of False. A massage therapist can not bill higher rates for insurance without repercussion.
True

67. True of False. Medicaid will pay a massage therapist. **False**

68. True of False. A massage therapist can bill an injured worker, in a worker's compensation case, for balances due.   **False**

69. True or False. You do not have to be a "Certified Medical-Massage Therapist" to bill or be reimbursed by insurance.   **True**

70. True or False. If Medicare does not reimburse massage therapists, then insurance companies will follow suit and drop you.   **False**

71. True or False. You can be paid by the supplemental/secondary insurance when Medicare is the primary coverage. **False**

ADDITIONAL QUESTIONS SENT IN OCTOBER 2007

72. In Ayurveda, points are called what?   **Marmas**

73. What is the exercise used to stretch the biceps femoris? **Sit ups**

74. If you touch the client in an inappropriate sexual way, what is this called?
Hostile

75. In psychosomatic theory which region of the body is considered "more male"? **Head and shoulders**

76. Which is the best way for getting off the massage table after a massage? **Roll to side with neck relaxed, drop legs off the side of table, then push up with arms.**

77. The stomach meridian in relaxation to the body runs in what direction? **Downward**

78. The therapist drops a pillow case on the floor, what should be done? **Place in dirty clothes hamper, then wash hands**

79. Where does the Conception Vessel originate? **Inside of the lower abdomen and emerges from the perineum**

80. The 3rd charka color is: **Yellow**

81. The muscle that abducts the humerus is the _____? **Deltoid**

82. Which portion of the large intestine passes through the pelvic basin? **Sigmoid**

83. There was a question about somata. The student does not remember the exact question. **NOTE: Somata comes from the word Soma meaning the whole body.**

84. The client of 50+years old has a family history of osteoporosis. She wants to prevent it. What exercise might be most helpful? **Weight bearing**

85. Heavy pressure on the mandible is contraindicated because it could result in what? **Sublimation of jaws.**

86. Which nerve plexus effects anterior arm b/w biceps and triceps? **Brachial**

87. In Massaging biceps femoris, the best position would be with a client in what position? **Prone**

88. Movement of the body toward the midline is? **Adduction**

89. This disorder is characterized by skeletal muscular atrophy in which the muscle is literally replaced with_____? **Muscular dystrophy**

90.   Crystalized Mineral chunks that develop in the urinary tract are?   **Renal Calculi**

91.   What is Homeostasis?

Homeostasis is a state of balance in the body. The balance is maintained through a series of negative feedback mechanisms.

92.   What is the study of the interactions between the nervous and endocrine systems? **Neuroendocrinology**

93.   Scoliosis is what kind of spinal curvature?   **Lateral**

94.   What is the Zygomatic bone?   **Cheek bone**

95.   What protein facilitates actin and myosin?   **Profilin**

96.   What is the synergist for the triceps brachia?   **Aconeus**

97.   A 40 year old woman radiation therapy survivor of breast cancer can have problems with?

    a.   bone metrix pericarditis

    b.   exophageal eflux

    c.   osteomalacia

    d.   tendon synoviitis

98.   What is dermatome?

A sensory segment of the skin supplied by a specific nerve root.

99.   What is allostasis? **The ability of nervous system to be resilient and to recover from stress.?**

100.   What vitamin is in the eye or what vitamin gel can help the eyes?   **Rhodopsin VITAMIN A**

101.   Can infection be a response to stress?   **Yes**

102.   What exercise is used to stretch the biceps femoris?

While standing, place a barbell across the back of your shoulders as you would for squats. Keeping your legs rigid, bend forward at the waist, with head up, until your upper body is parallel with the floor. Reverse the movement to bring your upper body back up.

103. What do you do with a client that you've been seeing for several sessions who has become repulsive to you lately?
      Ask your instructor as there are several different answers that are given on the exam.

104. What taste goes with the spleen? **Sweet or sour**

105. If the medial side of the foot drops what would this be called? **Pigeon toe**

106. If you are in a two-car accident, how would people go about getting the copy of the records of the accident? **At a police station after having filed a report.**

107. If a client complains of dry eyes and blurry vision, what meridian is out of balance? **Liver**

108. The zebra striped pattern is called? **A dermatome**

109. The stomach's yin/yang relationship to another organ is? **Spleen (yin)**

110. Myelin is associated with? **Insulation**

111. Which is distal to the olecranon process?

112. Which is proximal to the brachial plexus?

113. You should not apply deep pressure to the cubitalarea due to? **Brachial artery**

114. The stomach meridian begins where? **Under the pupil of the eye and turns up.....**

115. Where is the governing Vessel? **The governing vessel begins in the pelvic cavity, and ascends along the middle of the spinal column to penetrate the brain**

116. The Sciatic nerve passes through which two palpable bony structures? **Hip, and the gluteal region and sometimes through the piriformis**

117. Which of the following muscles cross two joints? **Gastrocnemius**

118. How would you position a client with lordosis?

   Put a pillow or towel or even a bolster under the belly to get rid of the exaggeration of the lordotic curve.

119. What kind of fluid would you find in the joints? **Synovial**

120. What would be the best relief treatment for someone with chronic Rheumatoid arthritis?

   Moist heat

Additional Questions Sent in from March to May 2007

1. An alcoholic client would show what in Chinese element. **Wood**

2. What type of stretch would you use for joint pain? **Rhythmic initiation stretch**

3. Adult blood cells are made from what? **Red or yellow marrow? Red marrow**

4. What is the connective tissue layer covering the entire muscle? **Epimysium**

5. What is the only bilateral joint? **Saddle joint (the thumb)**

6. What holds the body together? **Fascia**

7. Homeostasis influences what system? **Endocrine**

8. In Chinese medicine, Jing influences what system? **Reproductive system**

9. Which of these two vitamins, B & C, is water soluble? **Both**

10. What amino acid breaks down carbohydrates? **Amylase enzyme**

11. What nutrient helps with clotting? **Calcium**

12. What is the action of the masseter muscle, what does it do? **Elevates mandible**

13. What is cortisol? **A hormone for the sympathetic nervous system**

14. In Chinese medicine, what is the middle burner?   **Digestion**

15. What are three steps to help clients navigate through chronic pain?
    1. **Understand the emotional dimension of chronic pain.**
    2. **Create a safe space for healing.**
    3. **Help client to utilize other healing resources.**

16. What two functions are muscle cells limited to?   **Contraction and relaxation**

17. True or False. Music affects not only our minds, but the body as a whole.
    True

18. What is perfect posture?   **A condition where body mass is evenly distributed and balance is easily maintained during standing and locomotion.**

19. What is the best way to wash your hands?   **Use warm running water with liquid soap and then dry hands with paper towels.**

20. What are five steps that can be taken to safeguard yourself and your business from law suits?

    Acceptance, planning, implementation, monitoring and reaction

21. What technique would you use to help alleviate bronchitis symptoms?
    Cupping

22. True or False. Traditional Thai Massage is shown to reduce pain levels and pain perceptions in patients with non-special low back pain, more than a joint mobilization treatment.   **True**

23. What type of therapy would you suggest for someone who wants to change a movement pattern?

    Feldenkrais

24. After changing treatment plans several times without a change in outcome, how would you continue?   **Refer person to another professional that could possibly help**

25. Which of these is trained to treat a subluxation?
    a. **Chiropractor**
    b. Podiatrist

26. What does SOAP stand for?   **Subjective, Objective, Assessment, Plan**

27. Which muscles are involved in hip hiking?   **Quadratus lumborum**

28. When would you use CPR?   **Cardiac Arrest**

29. What is the color and organ related to the 4ᵗʰ Chakra?   **Heart and Green (sometimes pink)**

30. What does the manual stretching of muscles and fascia create and promote.

    Creates mechanical, bioelectrical and biochemical responses that promote improved vascular and lymphatic circulation, increased oxygenation, removal of body toxins and a more efficient nervous system.

31. What is one of the reasons for elevating the lower extremity after a strain in acute stage?

    To reduce swelling around the injured area

32. What should you declare in barter?   **100% of the value**

33. Which muscle is involved in a sciatic nerve pain?   **Piriformis**

34. What are the muscles usually involved in shin splint?

    Longus muscle & tibialis anterior muscle

35. If a marathon runner, after his run, has a high fever, his skin is hot, wet and his heart rate is high, what is the runner suffering from?   **Heat stroke**

36. At what bony landmark would you locate the kidneys?   **12ᵗʰ thoracic**

37. Which items can be deductible for the IRS?   **Business in a home**

38. What color is the chakra for the thyroid?   **Sky blue.**

    Please go to the web site listed below as it has all the chakras, locations, colors and physical and spiritual qualities: http://www.spiritofangels.com/spiritofangels/chakrainfo.html

39. Which muscles are working when riding a bicycle?   **Trunk muscles Quadriceps**

40.   What are the four primary headache types?

Tension-type, Migraine, Coexisting Migraine and Tension-type, Cluster

41.   What is the first vertebra? **Atlas**

42.   If you volunteer at a sports event and work as a massage therapist what can be deducted on your federal tax? **Non deductible**

43.   When implementing tapping techniques, what specific points are being tapped?

Acupuncture points, chakras, or other energy centers

44.   Why are tapping techniques used?

To move and balance energy in order for the body to heal itself more quickly and effectively.

45.   True or False. Massage therapists should accept tips but not expect them.
True

46.   Where is the best place to palpate the sacrotuberous ligament?

greater trochanter, lesser trochanter, asis, psis but check sites on Google.com

http://www.lhup.edu/yingram/jennifer/webpage/hip_motions.htm

47.   True or False. Massage Therapy helps to decrease blood pressure. **False**

Ref: Massage and Bodywork Magazine Feb/Mar 07 issue

48.   What two types of massage affect both diastolic and systolic blood pressure?

Trigger point and sports massage increase both diastolic and systolic

49.   Where does the heart meridian end? **At the tip of little finger**

50.   Where does the lung meridian end? **Corner of base of the thumb nail**

51.   What is Zong Qi? **Chinese Poetry**

52.   What is Zhong Qi? **Chinese Calendrics**

53.   What is Zhen Qi? **Chinese Herbal Supplement**

54.   What is Wei Qi? **It is the superficial defense energy.**

55.   Which organs are associated with the metal element? **Lung/large intestine**

56.   Which of these organs is considered yin? Liver, Spleen, Bladder, and large intestine.
Liver and Spleen

58.   What does the upper burner regulate? **Respiration**

59.   Where does the spleen meridian begin? **Medial side of big toe**

60.   With which feature is the heart meridian associated? **Tongue**

61.   Which direction does the governing vessel run? **Upward**

62.   An athlete complains of pain in the patella after an event. What would you massage to best help him? **Quadriceps**

63.   Scar Tissue formation is called? **Fibrosis**

64.   Which hormone is likely to produce pleasure doing a massage**? Serotonin**

65.   How would you position a client to stretch the Pectoralis major?
Abduct and laterally rotate the arm

66..   What are the defining characteristics of rheumatoid arthritis?
Joint are red, hot, painful and stiff

67.   What is the defining characteristic of rheumatoid arthritis?
Chronic and acute systemic inflammation

68.   In Western anatomical position, where is the distal ulna? **Medial wrist**

69.   What type of movement does the radioulnar joint have? **Rotation**

70.   Contraction of which muscle can trap the sciatic nerve? **Piriformis**

71.   For which condition is moist heat contraindicated? **Edema**

72   What muscle is associated with spasmodic torticollis? **Sternocleidomastoid**

73. When palpating the insertion of the illiopsoas muscle, what structure should be avoided?

    Femoral nerve

74. An injury to one part of the body throws off the entire body. What is this called?

    Compensation

75. You are massaging a client who begins to have an increase pulse rate and breathing. This is likely a sign of?   **Anxiety**

76. Which is an eccentric contraction of the rectus femoris?   **Deep knee bends or sit-ups**

77. Give three suggestions you would give a client who has a Liver imbalance.

    Moderate exercise, small amount of sour in diet, rest, cut out sweets, fats and alcohol.

78. A supine client you have just finished massaging still has retracted shoulders. Which would you suggest stretching**?   Rhomboids**

79. For which of these is friction contraindicated? Bursitis, ligament lesion

    Answer: **Bursitis**

80. What is the stage that occurs during the first few days of injury, when there is pain, redness and swelling?   **Acute**

81. Two massage therapists decide to work together. What do they have to do to keep their taxes separate?   **K-1 form**

82. When is a gift certificate taxable?   **When it is purchased**

83. Which involves the inflammation of the tibial tuberosity?   **Osgood-schlatter disease**

84. What is the best treatment for a client who has chronic constipation and what area would you address?   **Use gliding strokes clockwise on the abdomen-stomach**

85. What is the best way to turn a client?   **Hold the sheet at the edge farthest from you and have them roll toward you**

86. Is massage indicated for all scars? Yes or no. N**o, It depends on the**

healing process of the scar tissue

87.   Is massage indicated for edema?   **Yes** or no

88.   What is the term for inflammation of the sheath surrounding a tendon?
Tenosynovitis

89.   Massage may be contraindicated for a client who has_____.   Recent
myoardial infarction

90.   Which nerve stems from the brachial plexus?   **Radial**

91.   A client shows loss of mobility, tension and elevation in her right shoulder.
What could be the possible cause?   **Dislocation at the lateral clavicle**

92.   Which hormone is secreted by the pyloric antrum?   **Gastrin**

93.   What are the three most common causes of back pain?

Lumbar strain, nerve irritation, spinal stenosis

94.   What is Spinal Stenosis?   **The narrowing of the spinal canal.**

95.   When is gastrocnemius in the isometric position?   **Standing position**

96.   How do you massage the quadratus lumborum when client feels tired and is in
the supine position?

97.   What micro nutrient is necessary for hemoglobin?   **Iron**

98.   What is probably the symptom or cause of lordosis?   **Back pain - muscular
insufficiency of postural muscles**

99.   What nutrient is beneficial for the formation of teeth, bones, the nervous
system and aids in sleeping? **Calcium**

100.   Neuromuscular therapy focuses on ___ ___ ___ broad categories of health.
Biochemistry, biomechanical, and psychosocial influences

101.   What are the muscles of the rotator cuff? SITS muscle group. **Suprapinatus,
infraspinatus, teres minor, and subscapularis**

102. A client says he is fine although has hypertension, tense jaw, and muscle pains and spasms, etc. what do you do? **Work with him attentively and address symptoms as they come up during your session**

103. In Ancient Asian techniques, what is the word for transporting energy Qi? **Meridians**

104. To palpitate the sciatic notch you would find it where? **Medial Gluteus maximus muscle**

105. How would you work the anterior serratus? **Abduct the arm**

106. Define neuromuscular therapy.

    A comprehensive program of soft tissue manipulation that balances the body's central nervous system with the musculoskeletal system. It is used to evaluate the soft tissues in acute injuries, chronic pain or dysfunctional patterns of use.

107. What would you do first if a client came in with a recent injury with redness, swelling, pain and inflammation? **Apply ice pack**

125. If you see a client at a social event and ask them what they felt about the massage they had, what code of ethics does this violate? **Private**

126. What is the most important reason for taking a person's medical history?

    So you can discuss contraindications

127. What is the first document usually used during an initial session?

    Medical History Intake Form

128. Of these conditions: eczema, psoriasis, impetigo, which is contagious with person to person contact? **Impetigo**

129. As you watch a client walk from behind, you notice the left or right hip is higher and the right leg is rotated outward. What muscles may be shortened? Quadratus and lumborum

130. What is the emotion of the liver according to Chinese theory? **Anger**

131. If someone is having trouble with insomnia, and palpitations and forgetfulness, hat organ is this coming from? **Heart**

132. If someone is fearful, restless and had a tendency for edema, which meridian would you focus on? **Kidney**

133. According to oriental bodywork there are how many major meridians? **12**

134. In holistic therapy the concept is what? **The mind and body cannot be separated**

135. In laying a client on their side you would do this how? **Place cushion between knees, neck and in front of stomach**

136. If a woman has gone through menopause she may have what?

    Research this question
    - Thickening of epithelial cell walls
    - loss of bone matrix density
    - increase of progesterone

137. In assessing a client with joint pain or immobility, the best way to know is? **ROM**

138. What do you avoid with someone who has diverticulitis or spastic colon? **Stomach**

139. The pyloric valve is located where**? Lower stomach**

140. What should you avoid as a practitioner in session? **Wearing perfume**

141. What does yoga do? **Strengthens the body and clears the mind**

142. There is a question about a stretch or tear in a non-contractile tissue. What is this called?

    A sprain

143. If you volunteered your services for a charity how does the IRS account for it?

144. What is the first, most important thing to do during the intake of a new client?

    Listen attentively

145. Which of the following physiological changes occur immediately following tissue damage?
    (Research for the correct answer)
    - **Histamine release**

- **collagen remodeling**
- **increased fibrin production**
- **decreased leukocyle migration**

146. Client's shoe is abnormally worn down under the medial edge of the heel. Which problem would their practitioner look for?
- **drop-foot**
- **pigeon-toed gait**
- **over-pronation**
- **over-supination**

147. Which of these is contagious?
- **Acne**
- **psoriasis**
- **herpes**
- **hives**

148. According to oriental medicine, what are the three causes of disease?
Internal (emotions), external (the weather and pollution) and germs and diet

149. What are two other names for Meridians?
Channels and pathways; meridians are pathways which life force energy travels

150. Name some of the benefits of yoga. **Helps circulation, tones muscles and organs, encourages respiration, promotes energy and vitality**

151. How many major Meridians are there? **12**

152. In acupressure, what are the gateways to the Meridians?
The pressure points

153. What are tsubos? **Another name for pressure points; points on the body that connect meridians, and an area of concentrated energy along a meridian**

154. There are three techniques for stimulating the pressure points and they all work to restore the equilibrium and strengthen the flow of Qi or Chi. Name these three.
Toning - dispersing - calming

155.   What is 'scope of practice?'   **It is that which defines the practice parameters of a particular profession.**

156.   True or False.   You should use ALL pressure points on people who have High and Low Blood Pressure.   **FALSE**

157.   True or False.   You can use ALL pressure points during pregnancy as it helps the unborn child.

FALSE

158.   When you are working on more than one Meridian in a treatment, is it necessary to open one Meridian at a time?

NO. Do what is most comfortable for you and your patient.

159.   True or False. Therapeutic Touch is a massage procedure that applies a very deep pressure working around the connective tissue that wraps around the muscles.

FALSE. That would be Rolfing.

160.   Name 3 techniques used in Hatha Yoga.

Breathing & relaxing, various body positions, mental concentration, muscle control

161.   Why would sports/athletic massage be beneficial after a sporting event?

It helps to remove toxins stored in the tissues; restores flexibility and mobility, and helps to reduce the chance of injuries.

162.   Name 4 possible negative effects of exercise in sports/athletic massage.

Strains in connective tissue or in the muscle, an increase of metabolic waste build-up in tissues, spasms that restrict movement, inflammation and analogous fibrosis

163.   In sports/athletic massage name one reason why deep pressure is used?

It is used to deactivate trigger points and relieve stress points

164.   What is the longest, main meridian on the back?

Bladder meridian

165.   What type of energy is associated with toning, calming, and dispersing?

TONING is associated with weak energy. When you are toning you use an incense stick which warms the area (the point) and you hold the stick approx. 2cm from the point. Also to tonify at a pressure point, you would hold a stationary pressure for approximately 2 minutes.

CALMING - you would use your palm to cover the point for approximately 2 minutes

DISPERSING - to disperse energy (Qi) at a pressure point, apply moving pressure with your thumb or fingertip in a circular motion, or *pumping* in and out of the point, for about 2 minutes as this encourages the smooth flow of Qi along the Channels/Meridians.

166.   What are the four primary tools used in muscular/structural balancing?

Deep pressure, passive positioning, precision muscle testing and directional massage

167.   Where are myofascial trigger points found?

Located in a tight band of muscle fibers; and found in muscle tissue or associated fascia.

168.   Name at least 9 benefits of receiving massage therapy.
   - **Improves body alignment**
   - **Helps in the process of elimination of waste material**
   - **Improves the oxygen supply to cells**
   - **Improves relaxation of abdominal and intestinal muscles**
   - **Helps to relieve tension**
   - **Helps to relieve sore, stiff joints**
   - **Helps in the reduction of adhesions, and fibrosis**
   - **Helps the nervous system**
   - **Helps to relieve insomnia**

169.   Do most therapists massage by muscle groups?

Yes, however, it is not mandatory but highly suggested.

170.   Name two characteristics of nervous tissue.

Irritability and conductivity

171.   What is Ayurveda?

It is the ancient healing system of India, and incorporates the triad: body, mind and soul, and consciousness which manifests as earth, air, fire, water and space. Believes illness is an imbalance of body systems that can be revealed by taking the pulse and also by examining the tongue.

172.   In India's Ayurveda healing treatments and applications, what are the three doshas?

Vata, pitta, kapha (sometimes referred to as the tri-doshas)

173.   Name the functions of each of the doshas: vata, pitta, and kapha.

VATA- Bodily air, the subtle energy that governs   biological movement/breathing

PITTA - Bodily heat/energy that governs digestion, absorption, metabolism, body temperature, assimilation, and nutrition

KAPHA - Bodily stability, maintains body resistance, lubricates the joints, provides moisture to the skin, helps to heal wounds, and supports memory retention

174.   There are pressure points that you should NEVER USE on people who have high or low blood pressure and on people who are pregnant. What are these points and where are they located?

LI4 - Located on the back of the hand in the web between the index finger and the thumb

B60 - Located on the outside of the ankle between the ankle bone and the Achilles tendon

SP6- 4 finger widths above the inside ankle bone, just behind the tibia (never use during pregnancy)

K1 - Kidney 1 - you will find this point in the crease in the middle of the ball of the foot, where the color changes from the ball to the sole. Tonify with your elbow to stimulate the kidney Yin and to revive consciousness but NEVER use this point if the client has low blood pressure.

175.   What oils and herbs should you never use during pregnancy?

Marjoram, basil, marigold, myrrh or rue oils and NEVER USE bayberry, motherwort or devil's claw

176.   Where is governing vessel (GV20) located and when would you never use this point in a treatment?

The GV20 is located in the middle of the top of the head between the ears. You would NEVER USE THIS POINT if the client has high or low blood pressure.

177.   What are some of the benefits of using various oils in Ayurveda healing treatments?

Softens skin, reduces stress, calms nervous system, and increases the suppleness of the skin.

178.   What are some of the benefits of Aromatherapy?

It can enhance a massage or healing session on the mental, physical and emotional levels and has been used for thousands of years in healing rituals, religious anointing, and for medicinal purposes.

179. What are two inhibitory reflexes utilized in Muscle Energy Technique (MET)?
Reciprocal inhibition and post isometric relaxation

180. Pertaining to our body, what would be our first line of defense?
The skin

181. If you are having a session and the client wants mostly friction application, would you use a lot of oils and lubricants for friction techniques?
NO, oil reduces friction

182. If you are studying oriental and eastern modalities, you may be asked the following: what marma point helps with leg pains and sciatica?
The sprig point

183. What are marma points?
They are referred to as pressure points in Ayurveda healing.

184. What is another word meaning vascular headaches?
Migraines

185. Many times massage therapists encounter clients who have dreadful body odor. What is the best thing a therapist can do in order to help get the message across' to their clients without offending them?
Place a sign throughout their treatment facility that reads: "You must shower or bathe prior to your appointment for health and hygienic reasons.

186. What do the initials ICE and RICE stand for?
ice, compression, and elevation
rest, ice, compression and elevation

187. Yin/Yang is a philosophy about achieving what?
Balance

188. Points near the ends of a meridian are often the most powerful in removing what?
Blocks and in relieving pain along the course of that meridian

189. What are the seven fundamental lessons in Anma?
1.   Massage is not just about understanding techniques but polishing techniques as well.

2.   **Do not proclaim yourself as the 'healer.' Establish a rapport with your client.**

3.   **Learn to see the body through the hands and not just through the eyes, and always give Anma from Tan Den (the area just beneath the navel where the center of Ki (universal energy) is. It's very important to know how to breathe properly when working on a client.**

4.   **Do not use your intuition to make judgements until you've developed enough fundamental skills.**

5.   **"Imagination is more important than knowledge." Be cautious but don't be afraid.**

6.   **Always follow the flow of Tao (the way of nature), do not work against it.**

7.   **Center and balance yourself by harmonizing Yin and Yang.**

190.   Name the endocrine glands and the hormones they secrete.

testes = testosterone

parathyroids = parathormone

corpus luteum in the ovaries = progesterone

ovarian follicle = estrogens

thyroid gland = thyroid hormone [thyroxine and triiodothyronine]

pancreatic islets = insulin and glucagon

anterior pituitary = secretes 6 hormones: ACTH, TSH, FSH, GH, LH and Lactogenic hormone

adrenal medulla = epinephrine and norepinephrine

posterior pituitary = ADH and oxytocin

adrenal cortex = sex hormones, aldosterone and cortisol

191.   If a client complained of shooting pain radiating from the back into the buttock and into the lower extremity along its posterior or lateral aspect, most commonly caused by prolapse of the intervertebral disk, what could this *possibly* be a symptom of?
Sciatica, the inflammation of the sciatica nerve.

192.   What does the word *Shiatsu* mean?

Finger Pressure. It is a Japanese technique used to treat some illnesses and pain

193.   Boils are primarily associated with what type of bacteria?

Staphylococcus

194.   In massage of the lower extremity, is the patient usually turned from back-lying to face-lying?

It really depends on whether the patient prefers being massaged on the back first. The patient is not usually turned unless pathologic conditions are such that it seems best to do so.

195. If a client has hypertension and complains of being unable to sleep, what treatment would you apply?

1st, massage the neck and the back followed by total body massage, and a general light effleurage touch.

196. A client has had severe arthritis of the whole body for several years and there is a limitation of motion in her left knee; no   motion of the patella; and a flexion of deformity of the knee at 145 degrees; what would your treatment be?

You would give her a massage to mobilize the left knee.

197. It is necessary for the student of Oriental Medicine to first study the theory of the Meridian System. It is as important as the student of Western Medicine having to first learn, anatomy, physiology, and pathology.

The 12 regular Meridians (Channels) are listed in the order of vital energy and nutrient flow, with rare exceptions. Please list them.

1. **Lung (L)**
2. **Large Intestine (LI)**
3. **Stomach (St)**
4. **Spleen (Sp.)**
5. **Heart (H)**
6. **Small Intestine (SI)**
7. **Urinary Bladder (BL)**
8. **Kidney (K)**
9. **Pericardium (P)**
10. **Triple Warmer (TW)**
11. **Gall Bladder (GB)**
12. **Liver (Liv)**

198. Meridians are named according to (1) the organ that is controlled by the energy flow, i.e. lungs, stomach, spleen; (2) the function of the energy, i.e., GV, Regulating Channel (RC), and Motility Channel (MC); and (3) Yin or Yang. In a Yin Meridian, energy mainly flows where?

The location of the Yin Meridians is anterior, therefore it would flow outside.

199. Name two therapies that are used to release the flow of energy.

Polarity therapies and Shiatsu

200. What are the Yin organs?

Lungs, kidneys, liver, spleen and heart

201.   In Shiatsu, where is hara located?

In the abdomen

202.   In Ayurvedic assessment, what are the five methods of acquiring information?

Academic

Direct perception and inference

Questioning

Observation

Tactile perception

203.   The Principles of Unwinding is a term used in what modality?

Cranial Therapy

204.   Is Russian Medical Massage the same as Swedish Massage? Would the same strokes and pressure be applied to bring about relief of a specific condition?

No

205.   What are considered to be the two oldest and most foundational of the healing techniques?

Anma and Ayurveda

206.   Are Yin and Yang opposite forces or are they both positive?

Opposite forces

207.   Reiki is based on the principles of Chi. What is another name for Chi?

Energy

208.   What is the difference between isometric and isotonic?

ISOMETRIC means of equal length, when the force of the contraction is equal to the resistance i.e. when the ends of a contracting muscle are held fixed so that contraction produces increased tension at a constant overall length.

ISOTONIC means having equal tension, denoting the condition when a contracting muscle shortens against a constant load, as when lifting a weight, and when the force of the contraction is different from the resistance, and movement occurs

209.   What is Polarity Therapy based on?

A balanced flow of energy in the body is one of the most important elements for maintaining a healthy body.

210. Name a benefit of Therapeutic Touch.

Relieves pain and stress and balances the body's energy by applying a light gentle pressure, thereby helping the muscles to contract.

211. What does Chelation Therapy do?

Removes toxins

212. Define Rolfing.

First of all, Rolfing is an art, philosophy and a science. It is also a form of manual soft tissue therapy and movement education that is devoted to balancing and integrating the body in the field of gravity for the purpose of enhancing overall well being. It uses deep pressure and manipulation of tissues

213. Define Reiki.

It is an ancient healing technique that originated from Tibet. It uses a very light hand touch on key areas of the body to channel energy to those areas, providing a healing sensation or feeling of energy on those areas.

214. In oriental modalities the two vessels which travel along the median line on the front and the back are the two most often used for treatment. What are the 2 names and what type of energy is associated with each?

Conception vessel > reservoir of YIN energy

Governing vessel > reservoir of YANG energy

215. _____ is an acupoint or acupuncture point on the body that can be used for relieving pain, or to produce certain effects to the internal organs and/ or to relieve symptoms.

TSUBO 21

216. What are the three most modern massage methods based on Anma?

217. Name at least five contraindications for Shiatsu or Anma.

1. **Cancer or leukemia; it can spread if you do massage**
2. **Fever**
3. **If client has suffered from an injury or a trauma within 24 hours**
4. **If client has been drinking**
5. **If client has had surgery recently**

218. What consists of the eight-fold examination in Ayurvedic assessment?

Pulse, tongue, voice, palpation, eyes, form, urine and feces

219. What massage technique is used more than any other in the western world?

Swedish Massage, effeurage

220. Name three techniques used in Oriental massage practice.

Touching, listening, and asking questions

221. What is Carpal Tunnel Syndrome and what are some of the things that cause this?

Carpal Tunnel Syndrome (CTS) is an entrapment and compression of the median nerve due to postural and structural misalignment. Some of the things that cause CTS are overworking as well as straining muscles of the arms and hands, causing a loss of nerve conductively possibly leading to a loss of muscle strength. Also, constant repetitive movements i.e. playing musical instruments (violins, cello, piano), and court reporters complain of CTS, massaging, typing, writing all day with a pen or pencil while holding improperly.

222. Organs receive their autonomic nerve supply primarily from what?

The homolateral part of the nervous system.

223. What is Qigong?   **Qigong is vital energy of the body. Gong is the skill of exercises for the purpose of improving health and for healing.**

224. In Ayurveda healing what is another name for energy nerves?   **Nadis**

225. In the West Tsubos are also referred to as: **Trigger points**

226. Name at least three theories/methods that can be added to enhance the practice of Anma.

Yin and Yang - five elements theory - tsubo

227. What is Kei Ketsu?

Tsubo on the meridians directly connected to individual internal organs and supports their functioning

228. List at least 11 contraindications in massage.

Broken skin

lesions covered by a scab/s

person under the influence of alcohol

cysts

blood clots

warts

varicose veins

ulcers

hematoma

herpes simplex

hives

229. Would it be a contraindication to massage a person with cancer?

No.   Bodyworkers who are not yet trained or up-to-date of the special needs of cancer patients should help the client find someone who has expertise in this type of treatment. Be sure and let cancer patients/ clients know how beneficial massage is in the recovering process. Also, Reiki, Polarity or even a light feather touch massage is excellent. We all need to be touched. It is very healing.

230. What is another name for heel-spur syndrome?   **Plantar Fasciitis**

231. What is Pancha Karma?

It is a term used in Ayurveda Healing from India meaning the purification and rejuvenation of the body, mind and soul.

232. In addition to applying pressure on marma points, what else is applied to these points?

Various essential oils

233. What marma point sends energy to the colon, reproductive organs and bladder?

It is the _oorvee point_

234. What does the word Yoga mean?

Union of the body, mind and spirit, sometimes referred to as union with God

235. List at least 3 different types of fungal infections of the skin.

Jock itch, Athlete's foot, Ringworm

236. What is periostal massage?

It is a technique using trigger points that helps eliminate pain and delay development of the degenerative process in the joints, bringing about pathological changes in the periosteum.

237. What are some of the contributing factors to insomnia?

Stress, anxiety, physical pain and depression.

238.   What stroke is generally used when changing from one stroke to another?

Effleurage is sometimes referred to as a transition stroke.

239.   The most important thing you can do for your client, in order to maintain a professional relationship, is to be an excellent listener and keep all conversations confidential. Is this true or false?   **True**

240.   If you were to apply heavy pressure at the back of the knee and massage improperly, what nerve would become entrapped?   **Peroneal Nerve**

241.   What does TMJ stand for?

Temporomandibular Joint

242.   It is extremely important to know the endangerment sites on the body because of the possibility of injuring a client. What are some of these sites and where are they located?

Upper part of the abdomen under the ribs - abdomen

Axilla is the armpit where there are many nerves

Interior of the ear - notch posterior to the ramus of the mandible

Femoral triangle - bordered by the adductor longus muscle,

The inguinal ligament, and the sartorius muscle-

Femoral nerve and femoral artery in the groin

Popliteal fossa - posterior aspect of the knee

Upper lumbar area - lateral to the spine and inferior to the ribs

Ulnar notch of the elbow - referred to as the funny bone

Cubital area of the elbow - anterior bend of the elbow

Anterior triangle of the neck - bordered by the trachea,

Sternocleidomastoid muscle and the mandible- carotid artery

Posterior triangle of the neck - bordered by the clavicle, trapezius muscle, and the sternocleidomastoid muscle

243.   What is psychotherapeutic massage?

An alternative method for the treatment of stress utilizing both psychology and massage modalities by a practitioner

244.   It is very important to set boundaries in your own life and in your practice. What is one important thing you should *not* do?

You should never combine your massage therapy with counseling UNLESS you are a registered psychotherapist and massage therapist. Then the alternative (psychotherpeutic massage) would be used if you have the proper credentials, and you and your client have discussed the procedure you would be using.

245.   Name some of the factors contributing to the formation of our personal values.

Significant relationships with others, nature, spirit and God, meaningful experiences and life changing events.

246.   What muscles attach to the coracoid process?

Biceps, pectoralis minor, coracobrachalis

247.   What is the difference between tendinitis and tenosynovitis?

Tendinitis is the inflammation of a tendon. Tenosynovitis is the inflammation of a tendon and surrounding synovial sheath.

248.   What is the most *non-invasive* form of bodywork?

Therapeutic Touch

249.   What is Anma?

In Japanese it means = The art of Japanese Massage. It refers to the oldest known form of traditional Asian massage and involves stretching, squeezing, massaging and stimulating the body.

250.   When you are taking a client's history, what does the abbreviation SOAP stand for?

Subjective findings, Objective Findings, Assessment, and Plan.

251.   When a new client schedules an appointment, it is important for the body worker to have their client fill out an *intake form* in order to assess their client's needs and any unusual conditions. It lets them know what type of services you offer, just as you would complete a form when going to your medical doctor for the first visit. What are some of the questions & info you should have on your intake form?

Your credentials

Boxes where the client can make check marks ( ) to indicate

Yes or No to certain questions ---- questions i.e.: What are you wanting to gain from body work sessions? Are you having any problems? Have you recently experienced any major emotional, psychological changes, past traumas? Where do you hold your tension?

It is important to have a very detailed intake form.   Those are just some of the questions you should have on your form. Note: Example of Intake Form is in this book.

252.   The word acupuncture combines two Latin words. What are they?

Acus = Needle   &   Punctura = Pricking

253. In Oriental Medicine what are Gathering Points?

They are points that have a special influence on certain tissues, organs, energy or Blood.

254. Certain points are particularly useful in diagnosis. What are these points?

Back Transporting Points

Front Collecting Points

Lower-Sea Points

Ah Shi Points

255. What is the definition of a chakra?

A wheel of energy

256. In Chinese medicine what color is specifically related to the kidneys, lungs, liver, heart, and spleen?

kidneys, blue

lungs, white

liver, green

heart, red

spleen, yellow

257. Can blood glucose levels be improved with people with maturity-onset diabetes if they practice yoga?

Yes. The Yoga Biomedical Trust discovered this after doing a randomized controlled trial to study the effects of yoga therapy on diabetes.

258. What can cause irritation of the sciatic nerve?

Spasms in the piriformis

259. Is it contraindicated to massage a client with encephalitis?

Yes, if in acute stages

260. What is one purpose of elevating a limb?

To relieve pressure

261. When is the best time to apply sports massage after an athlete has been in a competition?

With 24 hours after the competition

262. What is another name for a stiff neck?   **Torticollis**

263.   What is the proper response to a client who reports depression and suicidal thoughts during a session?

Refer them to a mental health practitioner

264.   Name one result of stress.

Decreased immunity

265.   Is the sexual preference of your client considered confidential information?
Yes

266.   If a client tells you about sexual abuse, what are some of the things you should say to your client?

I'm sorry you had that happen to you. Do you have a support group that you are going to? You can then suggest that there are several groups that help people who have been sexually abused.

267.   Jin Shin Do is a form of acupressure that works by releasing what?

Two points simultaneously

268.   What constitutes an endangerment site?

It is where you would compress blood vessels or nerves

269.   What accommodation might be made during a session for a client with cystitis?

Frequent bathroom breaks

270.   When a client does not want to disrobe, what should a massage therapist say?

They will work through the clothing

271.   Is diaper draping a termed used only for infant massage?

NO

272.   What is the definition of keloid?

A scar that is thick, ropy in appearance, with excessive tissue build-up. It is also abnormal cell growth.

273.   What is one of the first things a massage therapist does just before beginning a massage session?

Wash their hands

274.   Client records are confidential except when....?

By a subpoena or directed by the client

275. What feeling is a client having if a massage therapist observes short, quick breaths and rapid heartbeat?   **Anxiety**

276. Be sure and know the four stages of rehabilitation.

    Calm spasms

    restore flexibility

    restore strength

    restore endurance

277. What is the definition of Kinesiology?

    Study of body movement

278. If you shake your arm or leg, what is one result you might obtain?

    Relaxed muscles

279. How much income is reportable to the IRS?

    All of it

280. Sleep deprivation has some consequences. Name at least three.

    Slow healing processes, fatigue, reduced mental capacity

281. What is lordosis?

    Exaggerated concave curve of the lumbar spine

282. What is one way to ensure a successful massage practice?

    Have a diversified clientele

283. It is important for the massage therapist to use their body weight when applying certain massage movements. What is considered to be the center of gravity for massage therapists?

    The pelvis

284. Why do most businesses fail?

    Under estimate of capital and expenses

285. Which leg muscles are shortened by wearing high heel shoes?

    Gastrocnemius and soleus

286.   What organ is protected by the ribs and sternum?

Heart

287.   If a client came to you and they recently had major surgery, should you give them a massage? What would be a reason/s why you should be cautious?

Massage can be excellent after surgery BUT DO NOT massage an individual who is on immunosuppressant drugs or who has blood clots. Immunosuppressant drugs are associated with patients who've had cancer surgery or organ transplants. Wait until they are off of their drugs and have, in writing from their physician, permission for massage.

288.   What are the sensory receptors that are stimulated during a contract/relax exercise?

Propriceptors

289.   In your first interview with a potential client, should you determine if they have a condition/s that would be contraindicated for massage?   **Yes**

290.   What is asepsis?   **the absence of pathogens**

291.   What muscle is referred to as the bench-press muscle?   **The pectoralis major**

292.   How would you define CFS (Chronic Fatigue Syndrome)?

A dysfunction of the immune system. Can be accompanied by swollen nodes, non-restorative sleep, muscle/joint aches and other symptoms.

293.   Alcoholism is considered, by some, to be a disease. If you were to diagnosis alcoholism list at least four indications.

memory loss

solitary drinking

neglect of personal responsibilities

use it to feel normal

294.   Define substance abuse.

Substance abuse is using any substance in dosages or in ways that were not intended to be used by the product or item i.e. food, caffeine, cigarettes, cigars, drugs (prescriptions and illegal ones)

295.   What is the definition and function of the lymphatic system?

The lymphatic system includes the lymph, lymph nodes, lacteals, glands, lymph ducts, and lymphatic. The thymus gland, tonsils, and the spleen are also a part of the lymph system. The function of the

lymphatic system is to collect excess tissue fluid invading micro-organisms, damaged cells and protein molecules. Also the lymphoid tissue produces lymphocytes (a white blood cell) that is an important part of the body's immune system.

296. What is the endangerment site in the inguinal nerve area?

Femoral Triangle

297. What is the endangerment site in the anterior neck?

Carotid artery, internal jugular vein, vagus nerve, and the lymph nodes

298. What are the tender spots on muscle tissues called that can emit pain to other parts of the body?

Trigger points

299. If you are massaging a client who has varicose veins, would massage be contraindicated distal or medial to the area of the varicose veins? **Distal**

300. What are the bony landmarks where the sciatic nerve passes through the hip?

Ischial tuberosity and the greater trochanter of the femur, bony knob at the top of the leg bone

301. What are the landmarks for locating the brachial plexus?

It is the region between the elbow and the shoulder

302. What is an example of unethical behavior?

Talking about one client's problems to another client

303. What kind of insurance covers hurting a client during a massage?

Malpractice insurance or Liability Insurance (reseach this)

304. What is the most important skill during client intake?

Listening

305. When you are massaging the upper aspect of the pectoralis major, what endangerment site must you avoid?

Subclavian artery

306. What is edema? **Retention of interstitial fluid due to protein or electrolyte imbalances, or due to obstruction in the lymphatic or circulatory systems**

307.   What pulls head towards chest? **Sternocleidomastoid**

308.   Would massage be contraindicated in edema?

Yes, if edema is the result of protein imbalance due to breakdown in the kidneys or liver

No, if edema is the result of back pressure in the veins due to immobility

309.   Yes or No. If you massage distal to proximal in the lower limbs, would that decrease edema in the lymphatic vessels?

Yes

310.   Would massage be contraindicated for a hematoma?

Yes

311.   List some of the benefits of aquatic exercising.

Improves cardiovascular fitness

Increases lean muscle mass

Decreases body fat

Increases Range of Motion in the chest and shoulder area

Strengthens the back muscles and the shoulder muscles

Helps to reduce stress

312.   Yoga is most noted for increasing what?

Flexibility

313.   Specific cross-tissue stokes used in Pfrimmer Deep Muscle Therapy stimulates what?

The circulatory and lymphatic systems by removing toxins; and it also facilitates cell repair.

314.   Where would a client report discomfort if they had diverticulitis?

Colon

315.   What stroke would assist in removing waste from the muscles?

The kneading stroke

316.   How do you recognize varicose veins, and work with varicose veins?

Lumpy skin, purplish color

Massage proximal to the affected area might be very helpful, especially superficial (barely touching) techniques. Never do a deep massage

on small reddish groupings of broken blood vessels that sometimes surround a small protruding vein.

317. What is an example of an ellipsoid joint? **Wrist**

318. Do radioulnar joints glide? **No, they rotate.**

319. Golgi tendon apparatus inhibits what? **Muscle contraction**

320. Does moist heat bring blood to the surface quickly? **Yes**

321. Why would you have a client breathe into their abdomen after an emotional release?

    It activates the parasympathetic nervous system

322. What does the term "window period" mean in reference to HIV?

    It refers to the time between infection and before antibodies can be detected in the blood

323. Is HIV a blood borne pathogen? **Yes**

324. Yes or No. Does HIV die quickly outside of the body? **Yes**

325. Can hepatitis B live outside of the body for up to 3 or more months? **Yes**

326. Does HIV live outside of the body for up to 3 or more months? **No**

327. Bells Palsy is related to which cranial nerve? **The facial nerve (the seventh cranial nerve)**

328. If a client is in denial about their pain and frustrations and can't seem to give you accurate feedback about their situation/s, would this be referred to as coping strategies? **Yes**

329. What are some of the things that Aromatherapy consists of?

    Breathing in or applying essential oils distilled from plants for therapeutic, aesthetic or psychological purposes to help treat conditions and diseases

330. What is the origin of the short head of the biceps brachii?

    The coracoid process

331.   What type of joints are found along the spine?   **Gliding**

332.   Why do massage therapists not work directly above pubic symphysis?
       That is where the bladder is located

333.   Name some benefits of using essential oils.
       They are mood balancing and have both uplifting and sedative properties.

334.   Which organ stores bile?
       Gallbladder

335.   What bodywork movement is used to break down the adhesion of a scar that is well healed?
       Friction

336.   What emotion is associated with the gallbladder?
       Anger - you can remember this by saying... "that just galls me."

337.   What emotion is associated with the kidneys?
       Fear

338.   What emotion is associated with the heart?
       Joy+mental shock

339.   What emotions are associated with the spleen energy and lungs?
       Over thinking and worry

340.   What are the bony landmarks used to locate the proximal end of the ulna?

       Olecranon process

341.   What does the ulna articulate with?
       The head of the radius and humerus above and with the radius below

342.   Is the iliopsoas a flexor of the hip?
       Yes

343.   What should a massage therapist refrain from wearing while working?
       Strong cologne or perfumes

344. Name the 3 classifications of joints in order of greater to least degree of mobility.

Diarthrosis , amphiarthrosis, and synarthrosis

345. What are some contraindications to warm water therapy?

Open wounds

Fever

Bowel incontinence

Severe urinary tract problems

Extreme high or low blood pressure

Tracheotomy

346. Does extension increase or decrease the size of the angle between articulating bones?

Increases

347. Where do you place the cushion for a client who is lying prone and has lordosis?

Under the abdomen

348. What is the definition of vasodilation and would friction or kneading cause vasodilation?

Vasodilation is the widening of the lumen (the space in the interior of a tubular structure such as an artery)of blood vessels.   YES friction and/ or kneading could cause local vasodilation

349. How do you position a pregnant woman during treatment?

Lying on her side

350. If a client's legs are uneven where else might you find unevenness?

In the shoulders

351. What muscles are involved in the flexion of the humerus?

The pectoralis major, anterior deltoid, and the coracobrachialis

352. True or False. Deep effeurage encourages venous and lymphatic flow.

TRUE

353. How do you massage a client with osteoarthritis in the neck: how do you massage them? **Light digital pressure along the cervical vertebrae**

354. Define bursa sac and tell where they can be found.

Bursa sac is generally found in connective tissue chiefly about joints and lined with synovial membrane to reduce friction and is found between tendons and bony prominences and other places where there is excessive friction.

355. What is the definition of hematopoiesis?

It is the formation of red blood corpuscles or blood cell formation

356. What flexes the hip and extends the knee?   **The quadriceps**

357. Is walking recommended in order to prevent osteoporosis?   **YES**

358. Is the pubic symphysis a bony landmark on the anterior pelvis girdle?   **YES**

359. What is the definition of isotonic solution?

A biological term denoting a solution in which body cells can be bathed without a net flow of water across the semipermeable cell membrane. Also, denoting a solution having the same tonicity as some other solution with which it is compared, such as physiologic salt solution and the blood serum.

360. What is the definition of isotonic contraction?

Contraction of a muscle, the tension remaining constant; since the contractile force is proportional to the overlap of the filaments and the overlap is varying; the number of active cross bridges must be changing.

361. If a client complains of suffering from constipation, where would the discomfort most likely be?

Abdominal area

362. In oriental medicine which pulse is used for diagnosis?

Radial pulse

363. A client who is interested in energy work could be referred to whom?

A reiki practitioner

364. What are some functions of the integumentary system?

Heat regulation, secretion and excretion, sensation, respiration and protection

365. What is the function of ligaments?   **To stabilize joints**

366.   When assessing a range of motion, what are three things that you would check for?

Passive movement

Active movement

Restrictive movement

367.   Why do massage therapists take client histories?

To determine if there are any contraindications to massage

368.   In Oriental Medicine, Chinese diagnosis is based on many fundamental principles. What are two that reflect the condition of the Internal Organs?

Signs and Symptoms

369.   Oriental medicine takes into account many different signs and symptoms. There is a saying in the Oriental diagnosis: *"Inspect the exterior to examine the interior."* There are four methods traditionally described with four words in the process of diagnosing. What are these?

Another way to remember it is SALT.

(See, Ask, Look, and Touch)

Asking

Looking

Hearing (include smelling)

Feeling

370.   In the method of diagnosis by *asking*, what are some of the things that the doctor and/or therapist should discuss with their client/patient?

The living conditions of the client

When the problem arose

The emotional environment of the client

Ask questions pertaining to:

Fever and/or chills

Change in stools and urine

Change in sleep patterns

Sweating

Pain

Phange in thirst and/or drinking

Change in food and/or taste

Change in thorax and abdomen area

Change in head and body feeling

371. In the method of diagnosis by *looking*, what would some of this include?

Spirit or vitality of the person, complexion, face color, (especially face areas i.e. a bluish color in the center of the forehead which would correspond to the heart); a red tip of the nose denotes spleen deficiency; very short chin indicates the possibility of kidney deficiency. Eyes are very important in the diagnosis. Different parts of the eyes are related to different organs in the body. An interesting note for diagnosis using the eyes (looking) is if you draw a line horizontally across the center of the eye, the upper part reflects the back and the lower part reflects the chest; also the right eye will reflect lesions on the right side and the left eye lesions on the left side. Breathing patterns, shape of muscles, tongue, channels, ears, mouth, throat, nose, limbs, body, and demeanor are other methods of diagnosis.

372. Define palpation.

Examination with the hands, feeling for organs, masses, or infiltration of a part of the body, liver, pulse beat; feeling, perceiving by the sense of touch.

373. What are 2 definitions of axis?

Vertebral column, the second cervical vertebra

374. What is the atlas?

First cervical vertebrae

375. How do you stretch the pectoral muscles?

Abduction and lateral rotation of humerus

376. Which stroke encompasses skin rolling?

Kneading

377. Which stroke is defined as a slight trembling of the hand?

Vibration

378. What could possibly cause a client (while receiving a massage) to have an increase of heart rate and respiration?

The client could have a memory recollection that had caused them to become anxious/fearful, and the heart and respiration increase could be a physiological result of their anxiety.

379. Define Reflexology therapy and Neuromuscular therapy.

Neuromuscular therapy relieves tender muscle tissue and compressed nerves that radiate pain to other areas of the body. Reflexology therapy uses certain points on the feet, hands, ankles that correspond

to specific organs and tissues in the body and by applying pressure on these points, it can help relieve pain and bring circulation to the corresponding tissues and organs.

380. Define CTS, Carpal Tunnel Syndrome.

It is an irritation of the median nerve as it passes under the traverse carpal ligament into the wrist. It causes numbness, weakness and a tingling sensation. Massage practitioners, court reporters, and individuals who use the wrist motion frequently are prone to CTS.

381. Our food passes through the divisions of the large intestine in what order?

Ascending colon > Transverse colon > Descending colon > Sigmoid colon

382. Is a cold application used in the treatment of tendonitis? **YES**

383. What is fomentation? **Application of moist heat.**

384. What is homeostasis?

It is the state of equilibrium or balance between opposing pressures in the body with respect to various functions and to the chemical compositions of the fluids and tissues. It is also the process through which such bodily equilibrium is maintained, and it is a modern scientific term that happens to describe quite suitably the flow of Ki (energy) within and among the meridians. The idea behind homeostasis is that dynamic systems (in this case the human body) naturally seek and maintain a condition of overall balance. Whenever an external force is applied to the system, at least one change must occur in the system in order to establish a new condition of balance.

385. What is the first thing you would do if someone is having the symptoms of a heart attack?

Call 911 and then make them as comfortable as possible by loosening clothing that appears to be tight, then elevate feet

386. The lower free edge of the external oblique is the inguinal ligament. What two bony parts would this ligament be attached to?

Anterior superior iliac spine and pubic tubercle

387. Define *Resisted Exercise*.

It is the activity of inhibiting muscle contractions initiated by the client.

388. What 3 things/symptoms can appear when a client has a flare-up of Gout?

Area becomes painful, hot and swollen.

389. Why is lymphatic massage good for sinusitis?

It drains congestion

390. What strokes are good for bronchitis?

Tapotment

391. The purpose of Shiatsu is to effect changes in the flow of energy in a meridian by manipulating the energy vortices called _____?

Tsubos

392. Four primary principles govern Shiatsu techniques. What are they?

The giver maintains the attitude of an observer.

Penetration is perpendicular to the surface of the meridian being treated.

Body weight rather than strength is used to allow the hand to penetrate into the meridian that is being worked on.

Pressure is applied rhythmically.

393. Define a herniated disc.

When a disc is herniated, the surrounding annulus fibrosis of an intervertebral disc protrudes and puts pressure on the spinal cord or on nerve roots.

394. The fluid which flows into lymph capillaries is derived from what?

Blood Plasma

395. Name one type of bodywork therapy that would help release the flow of energy through the body.

Polarity

396. Some contraindications exist when using finger pressure to acupuncture points. Where would you avoid using finger pressure?

Directly over contusions, scar tissue or infection, or if the patient has a serious cardiac condition, pregnancy and high or low blood pressure,

and children under 7 years of age should not be treated with these techniques.

397. What is the first symptom that one gets when they are afflicted with osteoarthritis?

Burning, stinging, sharp pain in and around the joints particularly in the hands, knees and hip area

398.   When someone is having an epileptic seizure what is the first thing you would do?

Clear the way of any surrounding objects that might be in the way and make it as comfortable for them as possible

399.   Can massage get rid of stretch marks?

NO

400.   The piriformis is a source of sciatic pain when entrapped by what nerve?

Sciatic nerve

401.   There are several abbreviations that are asked on your exams.   RESEARCH THESE.

ROM	**=**	**Range of Motion**
ANS	**=**	**Autonomic Nervous System**
CNS	**=**	**Central Nervous System**
COPD	**=**	**Chronic obstructive pulmonary disease**
ATP	**=**	**ATP, attending physician.**
ATP	**=**	**Autoimmune thrombocytopenic purpura.**
PCP	**=**	**Phencyclidine**
AIDS	**=**	**Acquired immunodeficiency syndrome**
CPR	**=**	**Cardiopulmonary resuscitation**
ELISA	**=**	**Enzyme-linked immunosorbent assay**
HIV	**=**	**Human immunodeficiency virus**
HBV	**=**	**Hepatitis B virus**
EDTA	**=**	**Ethylenediaminetetraacetic acid (edathamil acid)**
TMJ	**=**	**Temporomandibular joint (dysfunction)**
SOAP	**=**	**Subjective (data), objective (data), assessment, and plan (problem)**

402.   What are two *possible* signs of AIDS in the early stages?

Night sweats and chronic diarrhea

403.   Is it a good idea to consider, in AIDS prevention, that all body fluids that are wet could possibly be contaminated?   **YES**

404.   The following case is being used to illustrate possible choices that can be made using combinations of techniques from three popular systems, namely *Swedish Massage, Shiatsu, and Polarity (information from Beverly Kitss, R.P.T.)* There is also some additional consideration given for this case. One intention in showing a sample case is to indicate how well different methods can integrate with one

another. The case also offers pointers for expanding the number of choices and possibilities for practice. It is meant to encourage exploration in the application of methods. The case is not meant to offer stock formulas, as there is no way of knowing how to respond until one is actually present with the client.

CASE: Client: GENERAL FATIGUE

A 37-year-old woman complains of fatigue and irritability since the recent holiday season. She feels that she has been caring for everyone's needs but her own, and now she wants to give herself a gift of relaxing massage.

Possible Session

Swedish Massage: give general relaxing Swedish massage with special attention to areas of tension. *Polarity:* intersperse Polarity techniques with Swedish massage for stimulating parasympathetic nervous system, thus deepening the state of relaxation. *Shiatsu:* work feet and hands.

Additional Considerations

Each of our three sample systems has elements that can help bring forth the most relaxed response to the work. In Swedish massage, the tempo and rhythm of stroking and kneading often add to the comfort and relaxation of the patient. In the same way, the Polarity practitioner may use rhythmical oscillations and gentle holding. The Shiatsu practitioner may seek a rhythm harmonizing the pressure and release with the breathing of the receiver. The voice tone of the practitioner may convey certain feelings of warmth and relaxation. There may be a selection of music from which the receiver may choose a piece of special background music. Environmental elements such as heat, lighting, and ventilation should all be checked before starting the session.

Be prepared for the possibility that massage may free the patient to express previously suppressed emotions, for this is a common response and may be as therapeutic as the bodywork itself.

~~~~~~~~~~~~~~~~

405.   Name the four basic steps in a therapeutic procedure that would be specific to a client's complaint.

Assessment, Evaluation, Planning, and Performance

406.   What is the best manipulation for local deep massage of soft tissue?

Deep effleurage

407.   Does Ayurveda (traditional Indian medicine) include yoga practices?

Yes

408.   What is the name of the fascia that holds the nasopharynx open?

Pharyngobasilar fascia

409.   True or False. Most therapeutic relationships with clients should be Professional.

True. The client feels you can help and are knowledgeable when you act in a professional manner.

410.   What is Sjogren's Syndrome?

It is an autoimmune disease that causes muscle and joint pain and attacks certain glands. Some of the symptoms can include extremely dry eyes, mouth and nose.

411.   What style of massage has the most specific touch and direction of touch? Trager, reflexology, rolfing, reiki, etc?

Answer: reflexology

412.   What structure do you have to be cautious of in the femoral triangle area?

Femoral artery

413.   There are two separate circuits in the process of the blood flowing through the heart. Be sure you know the direction of flow of blood through the heart.

Vena cava brings blood in from the body to the right atrium and then out through the pulmonary artery to the lungs for oxygen; returns the blood from the lungs via the pulmonary vein to the left atrium out to the body through the aorta.

414.   What muscle is affected with the hiatus hernia?

Stomach - diaphragm area

415.   Name a few functions of the skin.

Barrier to loss of water and electrolytes

Protection from external agents

Regulates body temperature

Regulates blood pressure

Acts as sense organ for touch, pressure, temperature, and pain

Maintains body surface integrity by replacing cells and wound healing

Maintains a buffered protective skin film to protect against microbial and fungal agents

Participates in production of vitamin D

Delays hypersensitivity reactions to foreign objects

Indicates emotion through color change

416.   Would Golgi's tendon organ be a sensory end organ?

YES

417.   What is dyspnea?

Shortness of breath or distress in breathing, usually associated with disease of the heart or lungs, and can occur during intense physical exertion or at high altitude.

418.   How does lymph move through the body?

Flows in the lymphatic vessels through the lymph nodes and is eventually added to the venous blood circulation

419.   In massaging the chest muscles (example: the pectoralis minor or major) where would you place the pillows during the massage?

Under the arms so as to relax the chest muscles

420.   How does a therapist determine if their knowledge base of pathology will enable them to safely meet the needs of their current clientele?

First, it depends on the clientele. According to Ruth Werner, author of *A Massage Therapist's Guide to Pathology*, "If a brand-new therapist is working in a setting where he or she is seeing a lot of clients with complicated health issues," she says, "that person will – I'd like to hope, anyway, find out fairly quickly that more information is necessary.

421.   What is the MOST IMPORTANT, MOST PARAMOUNT thing a therapist should be concerned about with their client?

The client's safety.

422.   What are the five MOST IMPORTANT STEPS therapists can take to further self-education and ensure well-being for themselves and their clients?

(1) Be informed about infectious diseases so you can recognize them in your client and avoid further harm to others visiting the clinic, harm to yourself, and further harm to your client

(2) Join local, national, and international massage organizations

(3) Keep reference books, a medical dictionary, and other resource materials for quick reference about various rare and common disorders

(4) Subscribe to journals to be current with progress made in the field of health-related issues

(5) Read the health section of newspapers so you can stay informed of any local endemics and epidemics

423.   What is the Rosen Method known for and who developed it?

The ability to treat psychosomatic ailments and it helps clients discover their true selves. Marion Rosen is the founder of the Rosen Method.

424.   Define Hanna Somatic Education.

A system of neuromuscular education which requires the client to recognize, release and reverse chronic pain patterns resulting from injury, stress, repetitive motion, or habituated postures.   It is also a hands-on method which teaches how to relieve tension quickly, lengthen and relax muscles, reduce pain, and regain comfort.

425.   What are some of the benefits of teaching parents infant massage?

It can help the parents have a better understanding of how to deal with an infant who is may have colic or cries a lot, etc.

426.   Define Scope of Practice.

It defines the parameters of a particular profession.

427.   If you are a practicing bodyworker and you also sell products, this might be considered as what?

Dual roles

428.   What is the goal of the NCBTMB Code of Ethics?

a) o ask several questions on Oriental modalities that should only be given on exams for students who are studying to become Dr's of Oriental Medicine, knowing students will not pass their exams because these type of questions don't fall into the category of Massage Therapy certification, and have to take the exam again which allows the NCBTMB to make a great deal of money at the expense of the students lack of information they were not taught in a reputable school for Massage Therapy

b) To not reveal to the students the questions they did not answer correctly,

c) To protect the veracity of the profession and maintain the concern of each and every client, and

d) Other

(NOTE:) It is obvious to the student, we hope, that **the answer is (c)** but we did want to make a point on a) and b) which is what hundreds of students have complained to our publishing company and still do on a weekly basis about number a) and b).

429.   If you are working in an office where there are many therapists and there seems to be several complaints from clients about a therapist what would this be referred to as?

Conflict management

430. What are some of the terms of ethics and professionalism?

Supervision, ethics, peer support, laws, morals, professional demeanor, ethical principles, conflict management, listening, code of ethics, disclosure, right of refusal, integrity, listening, delivery information, power differential, standards of practice, delivering information, informed consent, confidentiality, professional boundaries, sexual misconduct, sexual impropriety, power differential, therapeutic relationship, transference.

431. Define Gross Income.

It is the income that is generated by business activities.

432. What part of the body would be affected in case of diverticulitis and what is diverticulitis?

The colon. It is inflammation of small pouches (diverticula) that forms on the wall of the colon

433. **Note: Know all aspects of first aid procedures and the order in which you would apply first aid i.e. check out the scene, responsiveness, call 911, EMS, tilt head, etc. This is asked on most exams.**

434. What is Insertion of iliopsoas muscle?

Lesser trochanter of femur

435. When you are lying prone, which of the following muscles on the back range from deep to superficial?

Erector spinae, serratus posterior, rhomboids, levator scapula, latissimus dorsi, trapezius

436. Stretching, pulling, etc. can help in what condition? Bruising, scar tissue or what?

Scar tissue

437. What is the wrong position for a client to be in with posterior varicose veins in lower legs?

Having a bolster in back of knees and lower legs is a "*no no.*"

438. True or False. It is very rare in the Far East and in China for a person to have Asthma.   **TRUE. The development of allergic asthma is directly related to Western life-style. The only time Chinese people get asthma is IF they adopt a Western life-style of eating, etc.**

439. Where does the absorption of the most nutrients and fluids take place?

Small intestine

440. Insertion of the biceps femoris is where?

Head of fibula

441. What three techniques are used in sports/athletic massage besides those used in Swedish massage?

active joint movements

compression

cross-fiber friction

442. Palpation of the psoas muscle could endanger which structure?

External iliac vein and artery

443. What is the meaning of Somatic Practice?

It is another term for many 'touch' therapies i.e. Swedish Massage.

444. Would the femoral artery be involved with an endangerment site?

YES, it terminates as the popliteal artery

445. What affliction is torticollis and what part of the body is affected?

Wry neck, muscle contraction on one side of neck causing head to be tilted and twisted to one side.

446. Ileocecal valve is between which two structures?

Small and large intestines

447. What are three very meaningful questions that confront every therapist?

a) **What is the first thing I should do with a new client?**

b) **What would be the second thing I should do?**

c) **When have I achieved the goal/s for my client?**

448. What are some of the treatments that can be applied when a person has Ileocecal Valve Syndrome?

Rubbing a reflex area on the front of the shoulder (where the biceps muscle goes through a groove in the humerus) for one minute every other day for two weeks is helpful. It is advisable to go to an excellent D.O. in your area to check for nerve pressure as a possible cause.

NOTE: An open ileocecal valve should NOT always be closed. If you ate an irritating substance, your body in its wisdom may have opened the valve to get the harmful substance through faster. You should go

over your dietary history of the past two days before deciding on a treatment.

449.   What are some of the causes of ileocecal valve syndrome?

Any chronic irritation in the area of the cecum such as an irritated appendix from too much spicy, greasy, or refined food; not enough exercise, water, or any other unhealthful practice that will clog the lymphatic system) can cause spasming of the valve. Foods i.e. alcohol, caffeine, carbonated beverages, chocolate, char-broiled meat; incomplete   digestion from not chewing well, eating too frequently, overeating, dysfunction of the stomach or small intestine, etc. can cause dysfunction of the valve.

Any irritation in the small intestine, strong emotional upset, and overeating a food you are allergic to can cause the valve to become stuck open.

Nerve pressure in the upper lumbar spine can cause ileocecal valve syndrome.

Hyper or hypotonic psoas muscles can contribute to ileocecal valve syndrome too

450.   In what order is the "*normal way of walking?*"

Heel, lateral surface, then the toes

451.   What is synovitis?

Inflammation of synovial capsule

452.   What supports the inside of the knee by running vertically from the femur to the tibia and prevents the femur and the joint from collapsing medially toward the other leg?

The medial or tibial collateral ligament

453.   The lateral collateral ligament does the same thing for the outside of the collateral ligament except that its lower end attaches to the head of the

_____.

Fibula

454.   The lateral collateral ligament and the tibial collateral ligament prevent abduction and adduction of the _____.   **Knee**

455.   What is another name for the semilunar cartilages?   Menisci

456.   Of the abductor group of muscles, what three participate with the knee?

The upper fibers of the gluteus maximus

The tensor faciae latae

The gluteus medius

457.   What are the principal flexors of the knee?

The hamstrings

458.   True or False. Massage improves immune function in HIV-positive adolescents.

True

459.   True or False. Massage eases lower back pain.

True

460.   There are four horizontal planes to evaluate for physical distortion in Neuromuscular Therapy. What are they?

(1)   the cranial base

(2)   the shoulders

(3)   the pelvis

(4)   the talus joints in the ankles

461.   What is Zero Balancing?

It is a hands-on method to align body energy with body structure, by correcting imbalances between energy and structure that could possibly lead to loss of vitality, chronic pain and decreased potential for vibrant health.

462.   Can massage help reduce high blood pressure. **Yes**

463.   On the anterior medial side of the wrist, which muscle tendons are you palpating?

Flexor carpi ulnaris

464.   No pressure should be used around axillary area because of the _____?

Musculocutaneous nerve

465.   What are the flexors of the humerus?

Pectoralis major (clavicular fibers)

Anterior deltoid

Biceps brachii (short head)

Coracobrachialis

466.   What is the best massage stroke to break up area of fibrois (hard tissue build

up)?

Friction or deep effleurage

467. If your client suddenly takes a long deep breath and then starts breathing at a slower rate - why would this happen?

The parasympathetic nervous system has taken over

468. Full rotation in a circular motion of the wrist includes which motion? Pronation, supination or circumduction

Circumduction

469. What is the best manipulation for local deep massage of soft tissue?

Deep effleurage

470. Static pressure on patient who contracts muscle would be what? Choices are: isometric, isotonic, etc.

Isometric

471. What do shiatsu, acupuncture, and anma therapy have in common?

They use pressure points

472. What system protects the body, excretes waste, and regulates temperature?

Integumentary system

473. If you are massaging a client and that client wants you to squeeze a pimple or blackhead, what would you tell the client and why should you not do this?

You should never squeeze a pimple

This is not within Scope of Practice

474. What is a Yoga Asana?

A pose, i.e. standing, inverted, backward and forward bending.

475. Which stroke would most effectively address *adhesion in tendinous tissue?*

Friction

476. What would describe the effects of fascial adhesions?

Decreased muscle power w/increased chance of injury

477. Which hormone stimulates retention of water by the kidneys?

ADH (antidiuretic hormone)

478.   There are two main classifications of glands. Please name the two glands.

Duct glands/exocrine and the ductless glands/endocrine

479.   Which organ is located in the upper right quadrant of the body?

Liver

480.   Which organ is located in the upper left area below the ribs?

Spleen

481.   This is a two part question.

(A) There are five elements that represent the qualities of ki energy. What are they?

wood, metal, water

earth and fire

(B) Which muscle originates at the sacrum, inserts on the greater trochanter, and is an external rotator of the hip?

Piriformis

482.   Abdominal inhalation requires contraction of which of the following muscles?

Answer: diaphragm

483.   What hydrotherapy modality is used to decrease pain and cellular metabolism?

Ice Pack

484.   The mastoid process is an insertion point for what muscles?

Splenius capitus, the sternocleidomastoid, and longissimus and diagastric

485.   The purpose of the pleural fluid surrounding the lungs is to do what?

Lubricate the opposed membrane

486.   In which abdominal pelvic quadrant is the sigmoid flexure of the colon located?

Lower left

487.   Digested food stuffs or contents are passed through the large intestine in what order? **Ascending colon, transverse colon, descending colon, sigmoid colon, rectum, anus**

488.   Which of the following best describes Psoriasis?

Chronic skin disorder (this appears but the question is worded differently)

489. The muscles of the posterior thigh from lateral to medial are:

Biceps femoris, Semitendinosus, and Semimembranosus (BTM)

490. The parasympathetic system is stimulated by what type of massage stroke?

Long gliding strokes

491. Name 6 important endrocrine glands.

Sex glands (gonads)

Pituitary gland

Parathyroid glands

Thyroid gland

Pancreas

Adrenal glands

492. Name one type of therapy that focuses on pain relief and explores the soft tissue components of pain.

493. Which bone is the lateral malleus associated with?

Fibula

494. What are some distinguishing factors of rheumatoid arthritis?

Fatigue, general discomfort, uneasiness, or ill feeling; (malaise) loss of appetite, low-grade joint pain, joint stiffness and joint swelling, usually symmetrical, may involve wrist pain; or neck pain, limited range of motion, morning stiffness, deformities of hands and feet; round, painless nodules under the skin.

495. The vertebral artery is vulnerable when doing what manipulation?

When massaging just below the mastoid continuing down the neck.

496. What are the muscles that move the mandible?

The movement of Mandible is done by: Lateral pterygoid- moves the mandible medially and forward; Left lateral excursion movement- Right condyle moves forward and medially; Disc- allows the condyle to move freely as long as the shape is maintained

497. How would you treat a client if they had tennis elbow?

Massage the extensor muscles of the forearm and the lateral epicondyle with cross-fiber friction, compression, deep stroking and soothing effleurage.

498.   When you are lying prone, which of the following muscles on the back extend from deep to superficial?

Deep layer: intercostals, rotators, multifidus, levatores. Intermediate layer: longissimus, erector spinae, rhomboid, serratus. Superficial layer: Lattissimus dorsi, trapezius

499.   If a client happens to fall just prior to coming to see you for their appointment and they injured their ankle and said they were in pain when they moved it, however you notice no swelling or redness, what would you do in this case or what would you suggest?

Do not work directly on the injury. Suggest they wrap the ankle and go see their doctor.

500.   Is it helpful to massage a client who has severe cardiac congestion?

Absolutely not.

501.   If a client comes in complaining of pain in their right shoulder from a car accident, which of the following would be an appropriate response?

(A) Have you seen a doctor? (B) Would you like an Aspirin? (c) Did you get the name of the person who hit you? (D) What motion creates pain?

502.   What structure would be endangered at the ulna humeral area?

The Ulnar nerve

503.   Name two tissues that line the surface of the integumentary system?

Epidermis and stratified squamous epithelium

504.   You would encourage a client to stretch_____muscle if they have Kyphosis.   **Pectoralis Major**

505   **Manual Thermal Diagnosis** is a highly effective technique where the therapist uses their hands as tools to feel the changes in surface temperature on each area of the body; from cranium, face and neck, to the thorax, abdomen, pelvis and posterior visceral projections. It is through these changes in temperature that gives the therapist some indications on zones of conflict whereby the therapist can begin palpating the heat-projecting zones.

506.   _____ is a modality that does not involve touching the client's body.

Therapeutic Touch

507.   The modality that uses the tongue, pulse, and hara (breathing) in the assessment is called _____.   **Chinese Medicine**

508.   _____ is the organ that is responsible for filtering old, dead red blood cells.   **Spleen**

509. Where does lymph return to circulation?
Subclavian vein

510. These 3 (perimysium, epimysium, and endomysium) form the structure of what?
Muscle fiber

511. The sciatic nerve is located where?
Gluteal region, hamstrings and lower leg

512. When palpating the popliteal fossa, the structure to be aware of is which of the following?
(a) tibial nerve
(b) popliteal artery
(c) common peroneal nerve
(d) all of the above
ANSWER: D

513. Tibialis anterior is innervated by _____?
Deep peroneal nerve

514. _____vessel goes from the heart to the lungs?
Pulmonary arteries

515. Is massage appropriate for an acute sprain/strain. **Acute is locally contraindicated.**

516. _____is the muscle used during normal, quiet breathing.
The diaphram

517. _____ _____ muscles are used during forceful inspiration.
External intercostals/serratus posterior superior

518. What is the correct order from lateral to medial?
(A) Biceps femoris, semitendionous, semimembranosus (BTM)
(b) Sartorius, gracilis, adductor longus
(c) Rectus femoris, vastus lateralis, vastus medialis
ANSWER: A (BTM)

519. _____is where you would place a pillow while working on pectoralis

minor.
Underneath abducted bent elbow, lying supine

520.   _____ would use scented oils and lotions.
Aromatherapy

521.   _____ would be the most appropriate technique that you would apply if a client had spastic colon.
Therapeutic touch/healing touch

522.   What is pes anserinus?
This structure meaning "duck's foot" is created by the convergence of the tendons of the sartorius, gracilis, and semitendinosus attaching to the superior portion of the tibia. Sometimes referred to as 'the bony landmark on the tibia."

523.   What principal are you using when you contract a muscle to increase its flexibility?
PNF Proprioceptive neuromuscular facilitation
Also this principal is sometimes referred to as Isometric Exercises

524.   Working _____ muscle dorisflexes and inverts the foot.
Tibialis Anterior

525.   You are stimulating _____ when you put one hand on the occiput and the other hand on the sacrum.
Cerebrospinal fluid motion or craniosacral motion

526.   Fill in the blanks: _____ muscle is palpated between the iliac _____ and the greater trochanter.
Crest (gluteus medius)

527.   Tennis elbow is best evidenced or indicated by what?
Inflammation and/or some tenderness of the lateral epicondyle

528.   Fill in the blanks.   All cartilages in our body have little or no _____ _____ and they tend to heal slowly.
Blood supply

529.   Which bone does the tibia articulate with at the ankle joint?
Talus

530. If you have been massaging a client and you notice that your client stops breathing, and after you have checked for responsiveness to make sure they are not breathing, what would you do next?

Call 911 immediately

531. Is crossing friction ever used in Russian Medical Massage?

Yes

532. Should your client, all of a sudden during the massage treatment, tell you they are experiencing some dizziness, complain of some pain down their left arm and some numbness, what is the first thing you would do?

Remain calm, get the client into a comfortable position and call emergency immediately (either 911) OR depending upon your geographical area, the fire department or police dept.

533. When working with the sternocleidomastoid what artery should be avoided?

Carotid

534. Define hara breathing.

Hara breathing is when the breaths are directed to the lower abdomen.

535. When you are working with a client and you begin to notice a very sweet sickening acetone like *odor* emitting from their body, what would you do, and what could be one possible cause for this?

You would suggest they see their physician because it could possibly be a sign of a *diabetic condition*, but remember you are *NEVER TO DIAGNOSE*.

536. If you are massaging a client and your client suggests to you that they would like for you to relieve them sexually, what are some things you can tell your client?

Remind them the purpose of Massage Therapy and you could also ask your client to leave. If there were problems you should call 911.

537. What is another word for *an unknown cause*?   **Idiopathic**

538. Red blood cells are formed in what tissue?   **Myeloid**

539. Pressure applied to hands and feet is usually done by a _____?
Reflexologist

540. How often are you to file your Federal Tax Forms, and how often do you pay your estimated Income Tax?   **Pay Quarterly and file by April 15th**

541. Why would you want to have Liability Insurance, and please give an example of what this type of insurance would cover?

Liability insurance covers a client falling or becoming injured on your property.

542. Why should you *not* place attractive throw rugs in your working area?

Client could trip or fall

543. What kind of stretching of the muscles can cause harm?

When using MET (Muscle Energy Techniques) the therapist should not use ballistic movements against the contractions when they are working with the client in stretching muscles (passive stretching)

544. Can massage treatments have a positive affect on cellulite?   **No**

545. What position would your head be in if your SCM muscles were contracted bilaterally?

The flexed position

546. What type of massage stroke would you use in the mandibular region?

Circular- friction

547. Please describe how to recognize a parasympathetic condition.

Watch client's breathing. When it changes and client takes in a deep breath followed by slower quieter breathing, this is the meaning of parasympathetic.

548. If a client complains of pain in the hip area and also some numbness down the leg, what could this indicate?   **Sciatica and piriformis problems**

549. You should be careful of what nerve when working on the sartorius?

Femoral

550. Joint movement is the strongest when the muscle attachment is near what?

Insertion point

551. If your client begins to perspire, this indicates that the _____ system is working?

Sympathetic

552. Other than Swedish Massage Therapy, what other methodology would involve

pressure point therapy at specific points while moving the hands and fingers in a specific direction?

Applied Reflexology

553. If you are massaging a client and they start to have an extreme anxiety attack, with profuse sweating and palpitation, what should you do?

Treat it as an emergency

554. What is diverticulosis and where would it be located?

Diverticulosis is a weakness of a sac opening out from a tubular organ or main cavity and it is located in the large intestine

555. When massaging the _____region you should be careful NOT to injure the musculocutaneous nerve.

Axillary region. This question has been asked several different ways on the National exam.

556. The _____ and _____ are considered agonist/antagonist.

Biceps brachii and triceps brachii. This question has been asked differently on the National Exam, i.e. What pair of muscles are considered antagonist/agonist?

557. If a person contracts a muscle and this muscle is pushing against static pressure, what is this considered to be? **Isometric**

558. One book states Yin is Dark | Night | Cold | Inside; while Yang is described as being _____?

Light | Day| Hot| Outside

559. If a client stops breathing and is unresponsive in a supine position, what do you do?

Call 911, open airway, give breaths, and check pulse (Standard first aid of course).

560. What is the anterior tendon that is the midway portion of the wrist near the crease, and what positions provide a full range of motion for the wrist?

Tendon of flexor carpi ulnaris and the positions would be: flexion, extension, pronation and supination

561. What organ is involved in the production of white blood cells? This question is also one that is in our study guides however, it is worded differently on some exams.

The spleen

562.   Name a muscle that spans two joints.

Gastrocnemius

563.   In Oriental Bodywork name the Yin organ that corresponds to the Earth aspect of the world.

The spleen

564.   What is the muscle that inverts the foot?

Tibialis anterior

565.   In reflexology, where is the point that corresponds to the neck and head?

Big toe

566.   What is the synergist muscle to the piriformis?

Gluteus maximus

567.   What is the main function of ligaments?

Stabilize joints - connecting bone to bone

568.   Why does injured cartilage take so long to heal?

Because it has little blood supply

569.   Name the joints of the pelvic girdle.

Hip, sacroiliac & pubic symphysis

570.   What is a likely contraindication for massage when massaging a client with diabetes?

Varicosis   (Varicose Veins)

571.   What extra considerations might you have for someone with hypothyroidism?

572.   What position would you place a client's arm while they are in the supine position, when massaging the serratus anterior?

Place pillows under the arms

573.   In what cavity is the psoas major located?

Abdominal

574.   What is Eastern Anatomical position?

Hands above the head, palms facing forward

575. How would you give physical support to a client in the supine position who had dowagers hump?

Pillow under head and neck

576. In the five elements of oriental theory, what organ is yang to the earth?

Stomach

577. In the five elements of oriental theory, what organ is yin to the fire element?
Heart

NOTE: Brush up on the oriental medicine applications

578. What two (2) muscles are antagonistic to each other?

Erector spinae and rectus abdominus

579. As a massage | body worker, what would be the best response to a new client who refused to fill out the client intake form?

Choose NOT to take that client. Approximately 100 letters that have been mailed or faxed to our company had this question on their exam.

580. In acupressure the pulse is taken to read the energy fields related to the organs. Where is the site in which the pulse is taken?

The wrist

581. What group of muscles are involved with the extension of the wrist joint?

extensor carpi radialis longus

extensor carpi radialis brevis

extensor carpi ulnaris

extensor digitorum

extensor digiti minimi

extensor indicis

extensor pollicis longus

extensor pollicis brevis

582. Name a bony landmark for the brachial plexus. **Clavicle**

583. Name the structure that inhibits muscle contractions.

Neurotendinous organs

584. What kind of neurons pick up information from receptors and send it to the brain and spinal cord?

Sensory

585. What kind of bodywork is a holistic body-mind psychotherapy which addresses the bio-energetic underpinnings of psycho/emotional distress; produces emotional releases due to the client's blocking of his or her experiences, and expression of life affirming emotions i.e. (anger, joy, fear, etc.)?

Reichian Therapy

586. What membrane is stimulated in joint mobilization?

Synovial membrane

587. What kind of joint allows movement in only a single plane?

Hinge joint

588. What organ of the body helps to regulate body temperature?

Skin

589. Which artery is used to take a pulse in oriental bodywork?

Radial

590. Which muscle would you work on if someone complained of patella pain?

Quadriceps

591. What is the 10th cranial nerve?

Vagus nerve

592. When massaging near the inguinal ligament what structure would you avoid applying deep pressure to?   **Femoral nerve**

593. When applying resistance to the knee while leg extended, what muscle is the primary mover?

Vastus intermedius

594. If you notice a regular client has a mole that has increased in size, what would be the best choice of action?

Tell the client you noticed it and refer your client to a family physician

595. What structure should you avoid when palpatating the tissue at the insertion of the biceps femoris?   **Common peroneal nerve**

596. What are some of the countries represented in TOUCH FOR HEALTH?

Canada, Mexico, New Zealand, France, Japan, Netherlands, China,

597. What hormone is produced to affect low blood sugar? **Insulin**

598. What is the name of the area of concentrated energy in a meridian line?
Acupoint or acupuncture points (small areas of high conductivity) or Tsubos

599. What organ mostly controls digestion in oriental bodywork? **Stomach**

600. What are the symptoms of anxiety or having an anxiety attack?
Very similar to having a heart attack; panic, quick breathing, can't catch your breath

601. A client has informed you that they have HIV and you are uncomfortable working with them, what do you do?
Acknowledge it, talk it over and come to a mutual agreement

602. In what type of bodywork does the practitioner apply static pressure with a low release and a stretch? **Neuro-muscular**

603. How would a massage / body worker address a client who has a peptic ulcer?
1st thing to do is ask if they are on any medication; 2nd don't massage around the abdomen area because you don't want to put any pressure near the ulcer, nor heavy pressure on the back opposite the ulcer

604. What type of massage technique would you use for a person with constipation?
Slight massage in clockwise direction over the intestinal areas

605. In what layer of the skin are vessels and nerves found?
Dermis

606. What are the five elements in Traditional Chinese Medicine?
Metal, earth, fire, water and wood

607. What is affected when a person has a sprain?
Ligaments

608. In Buddhist thought, what is YIN and YANG?
In Buddhist thought they are the two parts that contrast or exist as opposites of the same phenomenon

609. If someone was healing from a soft tissue injury why would you apply massage?
To reduce the build up of scar tissue

610. A runner has just injured his or her ankle. It is swollen, red, hot, and is beginning to turn black and blue. What would it be considered to be?

Hematoma or a fracture

611. What effect does massage have on urine output?

Has a tendency to increase the output

612. What is dermatome?

A segmental skin area enervated by various spinal cord segments; the lateral portion of the somite of an embryo which gives rise to the dermis of the skin; the cutis plate. ALSO it is referred to as "instrument for incising the skin or for cutting thin transplants of skin.

613. What organ is protected by the vertebral column & sternum?

Heart

614. What is idiopathic?

Cause unknown, no identification for a disease

615. If you sweat, what system is this?

Excretory system

616. What is diverticulosis?

A weakness in the wall of the colon that forms sacs or pouches

617. Most of our food is digested where

Small intestine

618. What is an inguinal hernia?

An indirect inguinal hernia in a child is a lump or bulge in the scrotum(boys) or groin(boys or girls) which contains bowel or other abdominal structure which has slipped through a persistent sac from the abdominal cavity. Inguinal hernias occur in 1-2% of boys and about one-tenth that often in girls. Up to 30% of premature infants develop an inguinal hernia. Hernias are most common on the right side but about 30% are on the left side and 10% are on both sides (bilateral). A hydrocele is a collection of fluid in any open part of the same sac and is closely related to inguinal hernia.

619. Where are the adrenal glands located?   **Top of kidneys**

620. To move the vertebrae in your back, would this be considered flexion and extension?

621. Where is the gall bladder located? **Upper right quadrant of the body.**

622. What are purkinje fibers?

The typical muscle fibers lying beneath endocardium of heart which constitute the impulse-conducting system of the heart

623. What does PSIS stand for? **Posterior superior iliac spine**

624. The apical pulse is located where?

In the 5th intercostal space, 7 to 9 cm to the left of the midline

625. Cold applications are use to do what?

Reduce swelling

626. What is the Heimlich maneuver and why is it used?

It consists of inward and upward thrusts on a person's abdomen, between the rib cage and navel, when a person is choking on a piece of food or other object. It hopefully throws the food or lodged object out of the persons mouth.

627. If a client comes to you for a massage and has a stoma, please describe what this is.

It is an opening to a colostomy through which the person empties fecal contents into a bag

628. What is a prosthesis?

A device such as an artificial limb

629. What is the normal range for pulse rate in an adult at rest?

60-90 beats per minute

630. Name the muscles of the back starting from internal to external.

Intercostalis, rhomboids, and trapezius

631. The extenders of the wrist are on the _____?

Lateral condyle of the humerus

632. Where is the origin of the wrist Flexors?

Medial condyle of humerus

633. If your client suddenly stops breathing what should you do?

Open their airway - give two breaths - call 911

634. Name some reasons applications are used in sports/athletic massage.

Deep pressure is used to relieve stress; cross-fiber friction is used to reduce fibrosis, compression is used to create hyperemia in the muscle tissue, and active joint movements are used in the rehabilitation of various conditions i.e injuries for rehabilitation of neurologic and soft tissue disorders, for Proprioceptive Neuromuscular Facilitation (PNF)

635. Which quadrant is the liver located in?

Upper right

636. What would help a client with osteoporosis?

Weight bearing exercises

637. What is above the pubic and is sensitive?

The bladder

638. What type of insurance would cover an injury in your office or your property?

Liability

639. What is the name for the excessive blood in the tissue area (reddened skin) in response to massage therapy.

Hyperemia

640. What technique in massage would move one layer of tissue over another?

Friction

641. Rocking and rolling techniques are used in what type of massage?

Trager

642. What treatment would be used for acute bursitis?

Ice

643. Shiatsu is associated with what type of pressure?

Finger pressure

644. Would an ice pack decrease cellular metabolism?

Yes

645. Give one reason why you would have your client fill out a medical history report?

To identify areas of indications and contraindications and other areas of concern prior to giving a massage

646. What is a secondary effect of using ice massage?

To relieve pain; 1ˢᵗ effect helps to reduce swelling

647. What are metabolic wastes?

Metabolic wastes are lactic acid and potassium that accumulate in the muscle that stimulates your sensory nerve endings. This build-up of waste by-products combined with the lack of tissue oxygen cause your trigger point pain.

648. Hot or cold would not be used with a person who has _____.

Neurologic impairment

649. What would be the best technique to promote lymphatic flow?

Deep effleurage

650. If a client seems depressed and discusses the thoughts of committing suicide, or happens to remember a childhood sexual abuse incident, what should you do?

Suggest they schedule an appointment with their physician or a counselor who specializes in those issues.

651. How much of the money you receive from your clients should you declare on your taxes/IRS?

All

652. What would the movement be between carpal bones?

Gliding

653. What technique would you use when beginning a massage session?

Effleurage

654. Where is the only saddle joint found in the body?

Your thumb

655. What muscles attach to the coracoid process?

Pectoralis minor, coracobrachalis, and biceps

656. Moist heat pack is contraindicated for the treatment of what?

Edema

657. What artery causes the back of the knee to be an endangerment site?

Popliteal artery

658. _____ churning occurs in the large intestines.

Haustral

659. Where is the mitral valve located?

It is the valve closing the orifice between the L atrium and the L ventricle of the heart.

660. _____is a skin condition that is scaly, flakes off and is usually red.

Psoriasis

661. What position should the client be in when working the iliotibial band?

On side with upper leg slightly bent and supported over the lower leg

662. Is impetigo a contagious skin condition?

Yes

663. Tongue and hara diagnosis are used by what type of bodywork?

Shiatsu

664. What should you avoid when you are doing a powder massage?

Inhaling the powder

665. How should the client's arm be positioned when you are working the latisimus dorsi?

The client should be in the prone position with their arm raised by side of head

666. What would you use instead of lotion or oil if your client has greasy skin?

Powder

667. If a client tells you that she is having a problem and needs to have her chakras balanced, who would you refer her to?

A polarity practitioner

668.   What acts as the stretch receptor?

Golgi tendon organ

669.   Where are the intercostal muscles located?

Between the ribs

670.   Name the condition that biofeedback is mostly used for.

Asthma and stress|anxiety

671.   When you are working under the clavicle what blood vessels should you avoid?

Subclavian

672.   What is a lateral curvature to the spine called?

Scoliosis

673.   Cluster headaches and migraine headaches are called what?

674.   Local application of cold produces what?

Vasoconstriction

675.   What are the two most common stances?

Archer and horse stance

676.   Contracting the neck flexors bilaterally would result in what?

Lifting the head while in a supine position

677.   If a client had chickenpox would this be a contraindication for massage?

Yes

678.   What exercise is good to increase flexibility and improve relaxation?

Yoga

679.   How would you position your client in order to relax the pectoralis major?

Supine position with pillows under the arms

680.   If a client had twisted their ankle before coming to you for a massage session, and they were limping but said that it was alright, what should you do?

Refer them to their physician

681.   If you are massaging a client and they "get out of hand and become threatening in any manner" what should you do?

Immediately leave your work area and call for professional help, usually 911.

682.   During meditation sometimes the _____ system is activated.

Parasympathetic

683.   What is a technique that can assess a weakness in a muscle?

Range of Motion ROM or Touch For Health

684.   Pain that occurs in one area but originates from another area is called _____?

Referred pain

685.   What is ischemia?

A low oxygen state usually due to obstruction of the arterial blood supply or inadequate blood flow leading to hypoxia in the tissue.

686.   Scar formation is called _____?

Fibrosis

687.   Where does a strain occur?

In the muscles

688.   What muscle is usually involved in *frozen shoulder*?

Subscapularis

689.   What organ can be palpated under the right rib?

Liver

690.   What should be avoided at the insertion of the biceps femoris?

Common peroneal nerve

691.   What is the name of the muscle that works against the prime mover?

Antagonist

692.   Where should heavy tapotment be a voided?

Over the chest area and over kidneys and on the back (if a person has an ulcer)

693.   Specific joint movements are caused by the _____?

Prime mover

694.   What are two very harmful foods that are making children & adults "hyper active"?

Sugar, any sugar by-products or foods whose name end in "ose" i.e. maltose, dextrose, etc. And white flour and any foods that have white flour by-products as an ingredient. The movie Meryl Streep starred in on February 16, 1997, on ABC told about a 2 year old boy who was having 90 epileptic seizures a day and was CURED after his DIET was altered. The two foods and by-products were eliminated from his diet.   It is important to research alternative ways to get off of drugs that have very harmful side effects, and usually a change in diet with proper exercise can produce what appears to be a miracle.

695.   What is osteoclast and what is it used for?

It is an instrument used to fracture a bone in order to correct a deformity

NOTE: Also, it is any of the large multinucleate cells whose function is to break down bone to maintain homeostasis and repair the bone.

The way this question was worded on the National Exam was very 'tricky' in that the correct answer would have been the instrument, not the cells.   Be very observant on how the multiple choice questions are worded. They are written in such a manner as to see how much you really have studied as well as how much you know.

696.   What is keratin?

A scleroprotein or (hard protein) albuminoid (a simple type of protein) present in hair and in nails

697.   Name 3 contraindications for hydrotherapy.

Lung disease, infectious skin conditions and kidney infection

698.   When the client is in the prone position the soleus muscle is underneath the _____?

Gastrocnemius

699.   Name an area where you would NOT perform heavy tapotements?

On the chest

700.   What is a prime mover?   **It is responsible for causing a joint action**

701.   What is another name for fat tissue?

Adipose

702.   What muscles are used when you grate your teeth, move your jaw and smile?
Medial and lateral pterygoids

703.   Name two things cold water application improves.
Stimulates nerves and improves circulation

704.   What part of the body should be raised when massaging the abdominal area?
The knees

705.   What does compression do?
It pushes muscles against the bones, and increases blood flow to the area, spreads muscle fibers

706.   Name 11 endangerment sites and their locations.
Inferior of the ear = notch posterior to the ramus of the mandible
Upper lumbar area = just inferior to the ribs and lateral to the spine
Axilla = Armpit
Popliteal fossa = posterior aspect of the knee
anterior triangle of the neck = bordered by the mandible, sternocleiodomastoid muscle and the trachea
abdomen = upper area of the abdomen under the ribs
femoral triangle = bordered by the sartorius muscle, the adductor longus muscle and the inguinal ligamentone
cubital area of the elbow = anterior bend of the elbow
posterior triangle of the neck = bordered by the sternocleidomastoid muscle, the trapezius muscle and the clavicle

707.   Name the six manipulations/movements that are used in Swedish massage.
Joint movements (passive and active) active resistive/assistive movements
Kneading (petrissage/kneading, fulling, and skin rolling
Effleurage/gliding (deep, superficial, aura stroking)
Touching (superficial and deep)
Friction (vibration, wringing, circular friction, cross-fiber/transverse)
Compression, rolling, chucking, and wringing
Percussion (tapping, slapping, cupping, hacking and beating)

708.   How are vigorous manipulations applied?
In a quick rhythm

709. Where on the body would you apply light manipulations?

Over the thin tissues i.e. behind knees, around the eyes

710. Where on the body would you apply heavy manipulations?

On the fleshy parts of the body and for the areas that have thick tissues

711. The word/s (terminology) of bodywork whether it be traditional methods, Asian, or Eastern the words for energy are what?

Chi, Ki, & Qi, and the word energy also.

712. One should never sleep with their head pointed _____ because it drains energy. _____ and _____ are okay, but _____ is the ideal direction.

South – it drains energy

East and West are okay

North is the best direction for the placement of the head while sleeping.

713. What is the origin of all forms of Oriental bodywork?

Anmo

714. List the Yang Organs.

Bladder

Large Intestine

Stomach

Small Intestine

Gallbladder

San Jiao (also referred to as the 'triple burner' because of the involvement of the San Jiao in metabolism   (burner meaning 'metaboliser).

715. List the Yin Organs.

Liver

Pericardium

Heart

Lung

Spleen

Kidney

716. What are the qualities of the three doshas?

Vata is responsible for all movement in the body

Pitta is responsible for all metabolisms in the body

Kapha is responsible for all structure & lubrication in the body

717.   What are Srotas?

Srotas, meaning channels or pores, are present throughout the visible body as well as at the "invisible" or subtle level of the cells, molecules, atoms, and subatomic strata. It is through these channels that nutrients and other substances are transported in and out of our physiologies. It is also through these channels that information and intelligence spontaneously flow.

719.   What are Marmas?

Marmas are conjunction points of consciousness in the body. There most common application is in Ayurvedic massage. There are 108 major marmas in the body.

720.   List the meridians in the body.

Heart

Small Intestine

Stomach

Spleen

Bladder

Kidney

Pericardium

Triple Warmer

Gall Bladder

Liver

Lung

Larger intestine

Central or Conception vessel

Governing vessel

Yin

Yang

The Five Elements

721.   Define Cun.

It is a unit of measure to locate an acupuncture point either on a human or an animal.

722.   Define meridians.

Channels of energy that flow up and down the body with relationship to the internal organs.

723.   What is cryotherapy?   **Application of ice**

724.   What is orthobionomy and who were two individuals who formalized and modified this modality?

Ortho-Bionomy® is a gentle yet very effective technique that eases stress and promotes relaxation. Working with the body's structure Ortho-Bionomy facilitates the therapeutic process and promotes natural body alignment, balance and pain relief. Ortho-Bionomy uses gentle movements, comfortable positioning and compression to restore balance. There were two doctors who played a role in this modality. They are Dr. Pauls and Dr. Jones.

725.   These are words you should become familiar with as the National Exam sometimes includes questions using these words that may apply to techniques, meridians, energy, characteristics, measurements, etc.   If you don't have the answers to these questions, we suggest you go to www.google.com and type in the word and become familiar with them. It is good idea to know the major characteristics of each meridian and organ related to the meridians and the names and locations of the major points used for various treatments on each meridian.   IT IS THE PUBLISHER'S OPINION THAT THIS IS RIDICULOUS BECAUSE TRADITIONAL MASSAGE THERAPY DOES NOT NEED TO KNOW MANY OF THE QUESTIONS GIVEN ON THE EXAM.   IF YOU ARE STUDYING TO TAKE AN EXAM IN ORDER TO BECOME A DR. OF ORIENTAL MEDICINE THEN, YES, THESE ARE VERY IMPORTANT THINGS TO KNOW. IT HAS BEEN BROUGHT TO OUR ATTENTION FROM A STUDENT WHO RECENTLY TOOK THE EXAM THAT THE NCBTMB LISTS IN THEIR 'STUDY GUIDE' SOME OF THE THINGS WE HAVE LISTED BELOW IN ORDER FOR YOU TO BE AWARE OF WHAT YOU MAY FIND ON THE NAT'L EXAM.

You may need to know the general characteristics of each element, what meridian they are associated with. Also we suggest you know the locations of the beginning and ending points of the meridians/channels.

- **Acupuncture points**
- **Nadi**
- **Kundalini**
- **Sushumna**
- **Brahmand**
- **Shiatsu**
- **Prana**
- **Dharma**
- **Ayurveda**
- **Cun**
- **Moxibustion**
- **Kyo**
- **Kitsu**
- **Tsubos**

- **Client and Practitioner agreement and policy statements**
- **Careet**
- **Reciprocity**
- **Deduction**
- **Taxes**
- **Ledger**
- **Budget**
- **Overhead**
- **Income**
- **Gross Income**
- **Net Income**
- **Expense**
- **DBA – Doing Business As….**
- **Croporation**
- **Sole proprietor**
- **Partnership**
- **LLC**
- **Mission Statement**
- **Burnout**
- **Law and Legislation**
- **Touch Techniques**
- **Diversity and Touch**
- **Gender Issues**
- **Erotic and/or sexual touching**
- **Advertising**
- **Business Cards**
- **Location of business**
- **Independent Contractor**
- **Licenses**
- **Records**
- **Paper Trails**
- **Bookkeeping Procedures**
- **Third Party Reimbursement**
- **Word of Mouth**
- **Brochures**
- **Dissociative Behavior**
- **PTS Post Traumatic Stress**
- **Mobility**
- **Prenatal**

- **Post Natal**
- **Credentials**
- **Banking Procedures for Business**
- **Receiving Cash for your services**
- **Start Up Costs**
- **Interview Questions and Procedures**
- **Intake Form**
- **Terminal Illness**
- **Things pertaining to physically challenged i.e. Visual, hearing, mobility, size**
- **Things pertaining to psychologically challenged i.e. trauma, psych disorders**
- **Things pertaining to wellness i.e. coping, nutrition, sleep, behavior, etc.**
- **Post Event – usually pertains to athletes**
- **Pre Event – same as above**
- **Restorative Massages**
- **Rehabilitation massages**
- **Remedial Massages**
- **Recovery Massages**
- **Trigger Point Therapy- Learn the major trigger points and methods of treatment**
- **Ambulatory**
- **Phantom pain**
- **Visceral**
- **Viral**
- **Idiopathic**
- **Congenital**
- **Anaplasia**
- **Malignant**
- **Somatic**
- **Bacterial**
- **Symptom**

Know the systems of the body. These include the following:

- **Musculoskeletal: bones, ligaments, skeletal muscles, tendons, joints, and the articular joints.**
- **Reproductive: ovaries, uterus, uterine tubes, vagina, penis, spermatic ducts, testes, prostate gland, etc.**
- **Cardiovascular: arteries, capillaries, heart, veins**
- **Urinary: kidneys, bladder, urethra, and ureters**

- **Digestive: tongue, teeth, stomach, mouth, large and small intestines, liver, gallbladder, pancreas, salivary glands, esophagus.**

- **Lymphatic: lymphatic vessels, thymus gland, lymph nodes, spleen and tonsils**

- **Respiratory: Nasal cavity, larynx, trachea, pharynx, lungs, diaphragm**

- **Integumentary: skin (largest organ), hair, nails, sebaceous glands, sweat glands, and breasts**

- **Know the groups of bones i.e. talus, cuneiform, cuboid**

- **Know the difference between the fractures: compound, open, complete, depressed, stress, simple, etc.**

- **Know the pathologies of the Skeletal System i.e.: clubfoot or talipes, cleft palate, osteoporosis, etc.**

- **Know the spinal curve abnormalities i. e. Lordosis, kyphosis, scoliosis**

- **The nervous system: brain sense organs, spinal cord, nerves.**

- **Types of movement permitted by diarthrodial joints i. e. flexion, extension, rotation. Remember to go to <u>www.google.com</u> and type in types of movement permitted by diarthrodial joints. You will see the list on one of the links.**

- **Also be able to identify the joint types, articulating bones, major ligaments and movements of joints i.e. Temporomandibular joint: Ligaments: lateral temporomandibular ligament, sphenomandibular ligament, and stylomandibular ligament.**

726.   What does the glenohumeral joint consist of?

Humerus and scapula

727.   How would you describe what an 'effort' is?

It is a force applied to a lever to overcome resistance.

728.   If you have been riding a bicycle for a very long distance, what nerve is sometimes irritated?

Pudendal

The Section covers sample Intake Forms, Contraindications, Business Practices, Descriptions of Various Therapies, Vitamins, Herbs, and Minerals

Descriptions of Various Therapies [1]

Acupuncture - is a means of contacting the electrical centers of the body and influencing the flow of energy (chi) to bring about a balance between positive and negative (yin-yang) forces. The energy or chi travels throughout the body by means of pathways called meridians. Needles are used to stimulate various points along these meridians. Massage and cauterization may also be used as stimulants.

Alexander Method - Fredrich Alexander believed that many illnesses can be traced to the way we use our bodies. Unconsciously, we have picked up poor body habits early in childhood from those around us. Also, stressful, urban life contributes to misuse of the body. The Alexander Method consists of techniques for unlearning the old habits so that the natural body can take over.

Applied Kiniesiology - is a system which is used by a primary health care provider to analyze our structural, chemical, and mental aspects of health. It uses muscle testing, postural analysis, gait analysis, along with other standard methods of diagnosis to assess and treat functional health problems as opposed to pathological health problems. Included in the Applied Kiniesiology approach are specific joint manipulations, various myofacial therapies, cranial techniques, meridian therapy, clinical nutrition, dietary management, and various reflex procedures.

Aromatherapy - is the enhancement of body, mind, and spirit with aromatic, botanical essential oils. The essential oil of each plant is its life force containing both medicinal and aromatic characteristics, and it remains potent and stable when properly extracted from the plant. These oils are obtained from the various parts of plants: leaves, flowers, bark, stems, berries, fruits, and roots. The oils provide tremendous healing and balancing properties when used according to proper guidelines. Most often used in baths, massages, and inhalations, they are readily absorbed through the skin and, when inhaled, they affect the brain and its release of neuro-chemicals. Depending on the essential oil used, aromatherapy can help you relax, enjoy, rejuvenate, increase mental alertness, and much, much more.

Aura and Color Healing - The electromagnetic field which surrounds the body is the aura. It is said that illness begins in the aura long before it reaches the physical body. A "sensitive" healer is able to diagnose by means of his/her visual perception of the aura. The affected organ or area shows up dark or grayish on the multi-colored aura. A color healer will apply remedial colors where a color deficiency exists or contrasting colors where there is an excess. Colors are applied actually or by means of visualization.

Ayurvedic Healing - is an ancient Indian science of life whose purpose is to allow one to understand his/her constitutional makeup and choose the diet and living condition best suited to his/her particular needs. This system uses only natural means of treatment and prevention of disease through herbs, oils, minerals, massage, heat, water, yoga, meditation, elimination therapy, diet, and life style management.

Bach Flower Remedies - Edward Bach believed that physical disease was caused by moods such as worry, fear, shock, etc. Bach used flower; bud, and twig essences in order to treat moods and thus disease. Specific flowers are suggested for balancing specific mind states.

Bates Lye System - This is a system for strengthening and developing the eyes. All eyesight disorders are seen as a result of strain that can be mental, emotional, or physical. In a relaxed state, the eye sees perfectly. Bad eyesight comes from chronic tension. Various exercises and techniques are practiced.

Bioenergetics - is a bodywork approach based on the premise that the body contains and expresses everything that happens to the individual. The body reflects who I am and how I operate in the world. Bioenergetic exercises are designed to open blocked or tensed areas of the body. As the body opens, so do the emotions and attitudes.

Biofeedback - Technological devices monitor the unconscious processes and feedback this information to the conscious mind. Thus the conscious mind learns to control the unconscious, to direct healing energy, and to restore balance.

Biorhythms - Your physical, mental, and emotional cycles all have a special and individual relationship to each other. By plotting and charting the physical 23-day cycle, the creative and emotional 28.day cycle, and the intellectual 33-day cycle, you can take full advantage of the individual energy patterns in daily life.

Chakra - is a Sanskrit word meaning wheel. The chakras are force centers or vortices through which energy flows from one of man's bodies to another. Disciplines do not agree as to how many chakras exist: some say 5, others say 7, and still others say 10.However many, all these wheels are perpetually rotating, receiving, and directing energies. There are corresponding areas on the physical body for each chakra: at the base of the spine, over the spleen, at the navel or solar plexus, over the heart, at the front of the throat, just above the space between the eyebrows, and on the top of the head.

Chiropractic - is the study of problems of health and disease from a structural point of view. Special consideration is given to spinal mechanics and neurological relations- disease may be caused or aggravated by disturbances of the nervous system: disturbances of the nervous system may have caused derangements of the muscular, skeletal structures. Chiropractic does not use drugs, medicines, or operative surgery in its treatment.

Colon Therapy - is sometimes referred to as colon irrigation or colonics or colon therapy. These are all names for the process which uses water for inner cleansing. Colonics are the gentle infusion of water into the colon-water goes in fecal matter is flushed out (the water is normally body temperature). A patient should always investigate the sterilization of instruments used by their colonic practitioner. The use of disposable rectal nozzles is obviously the most sterile. To a professional, health and safety must be of primary importance.

Cranio-Sacral Therapy - is a gentle method of evaluating and enhancing the function of the craniosacral system, a physiological fluid circulatory system that surrounds and protects the brain and spinal cord. This non-invasive manual therapy enhances the body's natural healing processes. It has been proven effective in treating a wide range of medical problems associated with pain and dysfunction.

Feldenkrais - Dr. Moshe Feldenkrais sees movement and the organization of movement as a key to understanding the relation of life style, self organization, and health. But even more important, Dr. Feldenkrais sees the reorganization of movement as a pathway to the kind of self reorganization resulting in the ability to lead a more healthy, stress adaptable, and efficient life. To this end he has spent the last forty years of his life developing a teaching based on awareness to help people learn to use themselves in less destructive and healthier ways.

Gestalt - seems to be a way of living rather than a therapy. Gestalt focuses on moment-to-moment awareness of the individual in all his/her detail and complexity. Gestalt is first a philosophy, a way of being, and then superimposed are ways of applying this knowledge so others can benefit from it.

Grof's Holotropic Breath Work - is a powerful technique of self-exploration and healing, based on and combining insights from modern consciousness research, depth psychology, and various spiritual practices. This approach is based on the mobilization of the spontaneous healing potential of the psyche in non-ordinary states of consciousness which are induced by breathing and evocative music. Holotropic Breath work mediates access to all levels of human experience including unfinished issues from postnatal biography, sequences of psychological death and rebirth, and the entire spectrum of transpersonal phenomena.

Homeopathy - was first formulated in the early 1800's by Dr. Samuel Hahnemann. Homeopathy's basic premise is that a substance which, in overdose, causes symptoms in a healthy person, will cure these same symptoms in a sick person when given in infinitesimal doses. However, before a homeopathist prescribes, the entire person, as well as the symptoms, are researched quite carefully.

Hypnotherapy - uses hypnosis as a psychotherapeutic tool. The altered state that occurs under hypnosis has been compared to a state of deep meditation or transcendence, in which the innate recuperative abilities of the psyche are allowed to flow more freely. The client can achieve greater clarity regarding his/her own wants and needs, explore other events or periods of life requiring resolution, or generally develop a more positive attitude. Hypnotherapy has also been particularly effective with stress disorders and various addictions.

Iridology- A means of revealing the pathological and functional disturbances in the body by reading the markings in the iris and surrounding areas of the eye. The iris is the most complex tissue of the body meeting the outside world. It is an extension of the brain, being endowed with hundreds of nerve endings, microscopic blood vessels, muscle and other tissues. Location of disease, its history and progression, and even clues to the cure, can be read in the eyes.

Kundalini Yoga - is the releasing of the coiled serpentine energy which resides at the base of the spine. This release is brought about by practicing a combination of postures, breathing patterns, mudras (hand or finger positions), and meditation techniques.

Macrobiotics - was begun over 70 years ago and popularized by Dr. George Oshawa who broadened the system to embrace the whole individual. He treated illness with natural foods and used no medicines. The diet is based on the yin-yang principle; all foods fall into one or the other category. If foods are properly chosen and combined, bodily balance can be restored in those who have fallen ill. Brown rice is said to he perfectly balanced between yin and yang. Proper or balanced diet is said to eliminate illness, fatigue, and to stimulate creative life.

Magnetic Healing - The healer attracts and transmits energy necessary to counteract the patient's disease. At the same time, the healer draws the energy associated with the illness from the patient. That energy is absorbed by the healer and later either transformed or shed. Most practitioners have favorite ways of ridding themselves of energy associated with sickness.

Mitzvah Technique - is a re-education and functional integration discipline, developed by M. Cohen-Nehemia, formerly of Israel, founder of The Canadian Mitzvah Technique Center and Training School. The technique is based upon a self-organizing ability, which is both preventative and remedial. Cohen's research and teaching demonstrates the body's self-organizing ability (seen clearly in young children) as an upward rippling motion of the spine with each movement of the pelvis-bringing with it a dynamic relationship between the pelvis, spine, and head, promoting spinal integrity. Habitual body misuse, occupation or accident, interferes with the pelvis, spine, and head dynamics, causing postural changes (eg., the chin pokes, the head retracts, the back hunches, the chest caves, and the body twists), resulting in diverse pains (back, hip, neck, shoulder, sciatica, and breathing difficulties). The Mitzvah Technique aims at restoring the body's self-organizing ability.

Massage - There are many different kinds of massage, but all of them touch the self or another in varying intensities of pressure. The contact can be used in a variety of ways: to increase the circulation by dilating the blood vessels, to stimulate the lymph circulation which aids in the elimination of wastes and toxic debris, to increase the blood supply and nutrition to the muscles and tissues, to improve muscle tone, etc.

Naturopathy - is a form of primary health care that has been practiced in North America since the turn of the century. Naturopaths recognize the inherent ability of the body to heal itself and act to identify and remove obstacles to its recovery. The naturopathic practitioner seeks to detect and eliminate the underlying causes of illness, rather than to merely suppress the symptoms. Naturopathic practitioners treat the whole individual, taking into account each patient's physical and mental health, genetic predispositions, and environmental influences. They also emphasize a preventive approach to disease and encourage self responsibility for health care. The Naturopathic approach can prevent minor illnesses from developing into more serious or chronic degenerative diseases. Patients are taught the principles by which to live a healthy life. The modern naturopathic practitioner provides a comprehensive range of diagnostics, treatments and therapies, and if necessary, referral to the appropriate specialist.

Network Chiropractic - is a network of many methods utilized in chiropractic today. Its practitioners view the spine as a powerful "switchboard of consciousness." In this approach, specific sequencing of both traditional light touch and structural chiropractic techniques are utilized. Rather than naming and treating symptoms and diseases, the practitioner locates subluxation at the spinal level and adjusts them. This frees mechanical tensions from the spinal system, empowering the innate intelligence to more fully express itself.

Neurolinguistic Programming (NLP) - is a comprehensive approach to developing more effective communication skills. It studies the different sensory levels through which we absorb information and how we organize, create, are motivated by, and make decisions, according to our own individual patterns of perception. Therapeutically, NLP has been used in work with phobias, learning disabilities, addictive behavior, and the development of new talents and more desirable, constructive behavioral patterns.

Polarity Therapy - This system views the body as a balanced electromagnetic field. The right side is charged with positive energy and the left side with negative energy. Too much positivity is associated with heat, inflammation, irritation, and swelling. Too much negative energy is associated with tension, spasm, and poor circulation. The aim of the therapy is to balance the energies in the body.

Posture Perfect - is a program developed by Robert Toporek, an advanced certified Rolf practitioner. Using the techniques and principals of Rolfing, Robert has taken the work of Ida Rolf beyond the traditional practice. The Posture Perfect program enables a person to undo postural patterns developed through a life of stress, trauma, and tension. In addition, this program addresses the patterns you have inherited and developed from birth. Posture Perfect gives you unimagined freedom in your body and life. By gently stretching muscle and connective tissue, tension and trauma are removed from your body. Through education you are given the tools to live into your new posture. People often report feeling looser, lighter, and being more productive with much less effort.

Rebirthing - is a safe and powerful breathing process that releases tension from the body, freeing it, so that we may live to our highest vision and unlimited potential. The breath is the ultimate healer. It is the umbilical cord to the

Claims Happen.

Liability insurance protects your career.

ABMP membership gives your massage and bodywork practice protection and a whole lot more.

The value of ABMP membership has helped us become the largest membership association serving the field.

Our industry leading $2 million per occurrence liability insurance covers you for professional liability (malpractice), general liability (slips and falls), and product liability (adverse reaction to a lotion). Add in legal defense, and we've got you covered. And it's occurrence-form insurance, which protects you from late filed claims, not inferior claims-made coverage, which expires when your membership does.

Insurance is just the beginning of your member benefits: you also get *Massage & Bodywork* magazine, a free website and e-mail account, outstanding practice-building resources, and a professional staff dedicated to serving you.

Insure your success with ABMP.

Associated Bodywork & Massage Professionals   www.abmp.com   800-458-2267

Ad sponsored by Insurance Facilities, Eau Claire, WI.

divine. By using a variety of smoothly connected breaths, energy which may be called Prana, Chi or Ki, or life force, is taken into the body dissolving and washing away anything that is contrary to life. When this takes place we become aware of our blocks and what has been holding us back; an inner cleansing occurs.

Reiki - is an ancient form of healing traced back to Tibet thousands of years ago. This technique was rediscovered in the 19th century by Dr. Mikao Usui, a Japanese Christian educator. Reiki is a hands.on, non-invasive healing technique. The word "reiki" is a combination of Japanese symbols when combined, present the concept of "Universal life-force energy." The client participates in their own healing. The reiki practitioner is a channel and a clear vessel through which the healing energy flows. Reiki energy allows us to heal ourselves spiritually, emotionally, mentally, and physically.

Reflexology - Strong massage of the feet at certain reflex points which correspond to the various areas and organs of the body. Reflexology points are different from acupuncture points. Foot treatments are said to dissolve the hardened toxins which accumulate in the body in the form of tiny crystals. Once the crystals are released into the bloodstream, they are eliminated naturally by the body. Circulation is increased and organs and glands are stimulated.

Rolfing - is an original and scientifically validated system of body restructuring & movement education. It releases the body's segments-- legs, torso, arms, etc- from lifelong patterns of tension and bracing, and permits gravity to realign them. By doing so, it balances the body. Because the body is better-balanced after Rolfing, it expends less of its vital energies against gravity. This biological energy-efficiency is often experienced as a higher level of alertness and vitality. Movement becomes easier and overall personal functioning tends to improve.

St. John Method of Neuromuscular Therapy - is a comprehensive system of soft-tissue manipulation techniques that balance the central nervous system (brain, spinal cord, and nerves) with the musculo-skeletal system. Therapists use these soft tissue correction techniques to restore proper functioning to muscles, which helps relieve pain and dysfunction.

Shiatsu - Finger pressure is applied to acupuncture meridian points by a practitioner. The pressure stimulates and balances the energy flowing through the body. A total body treatment employing the application of appropriate pressure to the meridians of the body according to the Oriental medical model. Pressure is applied mainly with the thumbs, but also with palms, elbows, and knees, to stimulate the flow of Qi (Chi or Ki), or energy, thereby promoting the self healing abilities of the body. A goal of Shiatsu is to facilitate a calming response and to maintain or restore physical function and/or relieve pain.

T'ai Chi - is a Chinese Taoist martial art form of meditation in movement, combining mental concentration, coordinated breathing, and a series of slow, graceful body movements. T'ai Chi may be practiced for meditative and health purposes or, with increased speed, the movements may be used for self-defense. The practitioner allows the body weight or center of gravity to sink into the abdomen and feet; this relaxes and deepens the breathing, quiets the mind and, in turn, regulates the heartbeat digestion, and various other muscular neurological, glandular and organic functions.

Trager Approach - is based on a simple concept: much discomfort, tension, stiffness and fatigue can be released by imparting to the nervous system a different set of signals. In this case, motion in the muscles and joints is used to communicate the sensations of lightness, ease, freedom, pleasure and aliveness. To experience these feelings in moving and being is to learn how to replace restriction with freedom in moving and being. These positive pleasurings are imparted (1) via gentle, non-invasive bodywork (psychophysical integration), and (2) through the teaching of simple, mindful movement explorations (Mentastics) which the client uses to generate these sensations on his/her own.

Unergi: Unity and Energy. A Holistic Therapy Method developed by Ute Arnold. It interweaves body awareness, movement, safe and healing touch, talk, dialoguing, inner listening, visualization and meditation, dream work, remembering, creative expression (especially visual art, music, and dance), ritual, accessing the woundedness, wisdom, playfulness of one's inner child, and attunement to nature; along with healing forms derived from Gestalt Therapy, Feldenkrais Movements, the Alexander Technique, and Rubenfeld Synergy.

Yoga - A spiritual technology or system whereby the practitioner can directly experience interior reality. The word yoga is derived from the Sanskrit, meaning to bind, to join, attach or yoke, to direct and concentrate attention on, to use and apply. Yoga techniques and postures often assist in adding flexibility to the body while focusing the mind. Click here for more Information on Yoga and Life Enrichment Network Yoga Instructors

Vitamins, Minerals, & Herbs

People report that vitamins, minerals, & herbs can be powerful and effective in improving health. Since they can interact in different ways with medications and since each person's needs differ, please check with your physician and/or primary care provider before taking. Also, make certain you follow your physician's or the company's dosage instructions.

Vit. A - Helps to maintain good vision, prevents night blindness, and dryness of the eyes; aids in growth, repair, and maintenance of body tissues. Helps form strong bones, teeth, and gum It is essential for pregnant or lactating women; it occurs in significant amounts in fish-liver oils, animal liver, eggs, and whole milk.

Beta-Carotene - Known to strengthen the immune system. Maintains healthy skin and eyes, prevents night blindness, and protects skin from ultra-violet rays.

Vit. B-Complex - A family of essential water-soluble vitamins which complement each other. Helps to combat negative effects of caffeine, nicotine, alcohol, antibiotics, fats, and sugar. Relieves effects of stress, strenuous exercise or improper diet.

Vit. B1 (Thiamine) - Important for metabolizing carbohydrates into energy and for normal function of the nervous system. Help in poor muscular and circulatory performance. Thiamine needs are increased during illness, stress, after surgery. Found in lean pork, beans, dried peas and nuts, liver, meats, milk, eggs.

Vit. B2 (Riboflavin) - Required for vision, growth, absorption of iron. Essential for healthy skin, nails, hair, eyes, as well as the formation of antibodies. Can be destroyed by light, heat, and air; it is often deficient in the diet. If you have cracks in the corner of your mouth and have light sensitivity of the eyes, you may be deficient in this vitamin. Found in beef, chicken, liver, salmon, nuts, beans and leafy greens.

Vit. B3 (Niacinamide) - Involved in hundreds of biochemical reactions in the body. Essential for normal body balance and the health of our nervous system.

Vit. B5 (Pantothenic Acid) - Essential for the synthesis of cholesterol and fatty acids and maintaining a healthy digestive tract. Important to normal immune system function. Deficiencies produce biochemical defects, retarded growth rate in animals, cramping and impairment of motor coordination. Found in the honey bee's "royal jelly."

Vit. B6 (Pyridoxine HCI) - Required for processing fats, carbohydrates and protein, utilizing linoleic acid an the production of antibodies and red blood cells. Lack of it may result in anemia, fatigue and hyper irritabilit. Found in bananas and raw steak.

Vit. B12 (Cyanoco Balamin) - Aids the normal synthesis of red blood cells and proper utilization of fats, carbohydrates, and protein. Lack of this vitamin may result in red and sore tongue, anemia and general fatigue,. B12 is absent from most fruits, vegetables, grains. Found in meats, animal products, tempeh, and other vegetarian sources.

Vit. B15 - HeIps increase oxygen supply to active tissue. Beneficial for those involved in strenuous exercise as it may prevent lactic acid build up.

Choline - Essential for the health of kidneys, liver, and arteries. A fat emulsifying agent which aids in the burning of intermuscular fat. Essential for normal nerve transmission, gall bladder regulation, lecithin formulation.

Inositol - Essential for the growth and color of hair, healthy intestinal activity, control of blood cholesterol, health of bone marrow and eye membranes.

PABA (para amino Benzoic acid) - A growth factor, PABA helps utilize protein and is important in the maintenance of healthy skin and hair.

Biotin - Aids in metabolizing carbohydrates and fats into energy. As a growth-promoting factor, it is important for the development of healthy hair, skin, and muscles. Found in liver, oysters, eggs, beans, peanuts.

Folic Acid - Essential in synthesizing DNA and RNA. Also important for the formation of red blood cells, protein metabolism, reproduction and growth. Lack of it may cause gastrointestinal distress. Found in spinach.

Vit. C - Essential in the formation of collagen fiber in the skin, bones, and ligaments. Beneficial against bone and tooth weakness. Lack of vitamin C may cause bleeding, swollen joints. Found in oranges, other citrus fruits, tomatoes, raw potatoes, raw peppers.

Vit. D -" Sunshine" vitamin. Essential for the assimilation of calcium, growth and development of bones, teeth, jaw formulation, maintenance of blood coagulation and cardiac rhythm. Deficiency symptoms may result in softening of bones and teeth, bone curvature in children, and calcium and phosphorous wont' absorb,

Vit. E - Essential for the assimilation of vitamins A, C, D, healthy heart and lungs, decreasing the pain in childbirth, utilization of oxygen by our tissues. Present in fresh whole grain wheat products as well as many cold-pressed vegetable oils. Deficiency symptoms may result in red blood cell breakdown, poor circulatory and muscular performance

Calcium - Essential for the transportation of nerve impulses, clotting of the blood, Vitamin C utilization, reducing cavities, formation of strong bones. Abundant in dairy products and in salmon (in the edible bones of the canned fish).

Iron - Vital component of hemoglobin, the oxygen.carrying pigment of the red blood cells. Essential for the production of energy and normal brain function. Important for stress and disease resistance. Found in liver, lean meat, eggs, and whole grain.

Magnesium - Nature uses magnesium to calm the nervous system. It is a natural sedative. May act as a catalyst in helping carbohydrates become properly assimilated instead of being stored as fat.

Manganese - Essential for normal reproductive functions, milk formulation, building resistance to disease and activating enzymes important for carbohydrate and fat production.

Niacin - Essential for the efficient use of protein. Lack of niacin results in intestinal disorders, mental depression, skin rashes. Found in liver; fish, lean meats and poultry, potatoes, nuts, and whole grains.

Potassium - Essential for balancing the system, controlling body fluids, normalizing the heartbeat, nourishing the muscles, assisting the kidneys' disposal of body waste.

Zinc - Aids in the digestion and metabolism of phosphorus and protein. Assists in burn and wound healing and in carbohydrate digestion. Essential for healthy skin.

HERBS

Alfalfa - High in chlorophyll. Excellent support for arthritis, rheumatism, colitis, ulcers, anemia, and osteoporosis.

Arnica - A first aid liniment for muscular soreness and pain from sprain, strain, over-exertion or arthritis.

Astralagus - Deep immune system tonic; improves adrenal glands function; useful in fatigue, frequent colds.

Barberry - For long-term inflammation of mouth, bleeding gums, sore throat; diarrhea from stress, excess food or dysentery.

Black Cohosh - Menstrual cramps with dull pains. Facilitates childbirth when labor delay is due to weakness, fatigue.

Burdock - Effective in dry and scaly eczema, psoriasis, acne, dandruff and boils; stimulates digestive juices.

Calendula - Internally: for peptic ulcers in remission; for varicose veins. Externally: for skin burns, healing ulcerations.

Catnip - Stimulates sweating in colds and flu. Eases stomach and intestinal cramps in children and adults.

Cayenne - Helps in viral infections, it cools dry, hot mucous membranes. Small amounts increase secretions.

Chamomile - Helps in anxiety, insomnia, indigestion, flatulence, gastritis, gingivitis, menstrual related migraines.

Chaparral - Helps in auto-immune and allergic disorders; also for people in long-term contact with chemicals, metals.

Chickweed - Externally as a rub for arthritis, strains, or gout. Useful as a diuretic for PMS water retention.

Chlorophyll - Low red blood cell count, fatigue, shortness of breath, high altitude sickness, heavy menstrual flow.

Collinsonia - Irritation of throat from intensive talking, singing, or shouting. Hemorrhoids and varicosities.

Dandelion Root - Poor bile secretion, appetite, digestive function; constipation from lack of bile; rheumatic conditions.

Devil's Claw - A safe anti-inflammatory for arthritis, rheumatism, gout, joint inflammation, and elevated cholesterol.

Dong Qual - For menopausal distress; in deficient estrogen or testosterone secretion; in PMS with dull aching pain.

Echinacea - Increases production, maturation and aggressiveness of white blood cells against intruders.

Eyebright - Internally for hay fever and allergies with watery eyes, sneezing, runny nose, stuffy sinuses.

Fennel - Eliminates flatulence. Very useful for babies with gas and distressed digestive system (e.g., diarrhea, dyspepsia).

Ginseng, Chinese Kirin Red - Most stimulating of the ginsengs. For physical or emotional stress or exhaustion.

Ginseng, Siberian - Substitute for "true" ginseng. Increases strength and endurance, resistance to infection.

Ginseng, Wild American - Emotional and physical stress, manifesting as elevated blood sugar.

Golden Seal - Helps in sub-acute or chronic mucous membranes inflammation, such as sinusitis, hay fever, allergies, gastritis.

Gotu Kola - Great support for thyroid gland where its low function contributes to emotional depression, dry skin.

Hawthorn - Helps heart irregularities with rapid heart beat episodes, or weakness of heart muscle from poor blood supply.

Hyssop - In pulmonary problems characterized by excess mucous production with difficult expectoration.

Licorice - An effective adrenal gland support. In gastric ulcers, bronchio-spasms, sore throat, painful menstruation.

Lobelia - Specific for bronchial spasms as they occur in asthma. Also, helps when trying to quit smoking.

Mullein - For coughs, especially of older asthmatic patients. Very useful in sub- acute or chronic bronchitis, emphysema.

Myrrh - in combination with Echinacea to elevate low white blood cell level. For painful ulceration of the gums or mouth.

Nettle - For hay fever. Tones up the mucous membranes especially with excessive mucous and inflammation.

Oats - Helps in the withdrawal of nicotine, cocaine or opiates. One of the best nervous system tonics available.

Pennyroyal - For late, painful, spotty menstruation accompanied by bloating, sore breasts and other PMS symptoms.

Peppermint - Stops nausea or vomiting; stimulates the production and the release of bile, prevents intestinal fermentation.

Pipsissewa - Bladder, kidney, or urethra irritation or infection especially after binging on alkaline foods, fruits.

Pleurisy Root - Useful in pleurisy, bronchitis or chest colds with dry respiratory membranes and skin.

Propolis - Mouth, gum, and intestinal infections; foul smelling diarrhea from intestinal infections.

Red Clover - High in minerals; good as a maintenance liquid during infections, hepatitis or mononucleosis.

Red Raspberry - In pregnancy, to prevent spotting in the first trimester and to increase muscle tone in the uterine walls

Red Root - Acute tonsillitis or sore throat; inflamed spleen and /or inflamed lymphatic nodes; fluid cysts in breasts, ovaries.

Sarsaparilla - Simple prostate enlargement; increases elimination of urea and uric acid. Helpful in gout, herpes.

Schizandra - Increases overall resistance. Helps fight stress, fatigue, tiredness, exhaustion and depression.

Skullcap - Inability to sleep, feeling on edge, restlessness; muscle twitching, neuralgia, sciatica.

St. John's Wort - Effective in depression, anxiety, agitation, insomnia, loss of interest and excessive sleeping.

Uva Ursi - Cystitis in paraplegics; acute cystitis and arthritis accompanied with sharp stabbing.like pain when urinating.

Valerian - Is helpful for insomnia, emotional depression, poor sleep from pain or trauma.

Yarrow - In fevers, common cold, passive bleeding of the uterus, bladder or lungs; gastric cramps, stomach gas.

Always consult with your health care practitioner. It is important to strive to find a qualified professional. Please make certain to search for the necessary expert advice and counseling for yourself.

[1] *We would like to thank Life Enrichment Network for permission to reprint the section of Descriptions of Various Therapies, Herbs, Vitamins and Minerals from their Internet address earthmed.netreach.net.*

SOME IMPORTANT CONTRAINDICATIONS FOR MASSAGE

You should be very careful and take a history of your clients before doing massage therapy. Many Spa's and Massage Therapists don't take the time to ask the client to fill out an Intake Form. It is imperative you know any conditions that may have a contraindication prior to giving a massage.

When a name appears and has no Local Contraindication, (LC) or anything by that name it is contraindicated (Always check with a physician on any condition in question)

Here is a list of some of the contraindications for massage therapy.

LC = LOCALLY CONTRAINDICATED

Abortion (no deep abdominal work)

• Aneurysm (not even if you suspect a client who fits the profile for aneurysms)

• Appendicitis, however after appendicitis operation it can be beneficial with Dr's permission

• Acne (LC, you don't want to spread the infection)

• Advanced atherosclerosis

• Baker's cysts (LC)

• Boils (LC)

• Bronchitis (LC)

• Bunions (LC)

• Burns (LC)

• Bursitis(LC)

• Cancer (should be done only with physicians approval)

• Candidiasis (LC)

• Cirrhosis (LC in advanced stages)

• Crohn's disease: (LC, some massage with physicians supervision)

• Cysts (LC)

• Dermatitis (LC)

• Edema

• Embolism

• Encephalitis (if in acute stages

• Endometriosis (LC)

• Epilepsy (during seizures)

• Erysipelas

• Fever

• Fibroid Tumors

• Fractures (LC

- Fungal Infections (LC)
- Ganglion cysts (LC)
- Gastroenteritis (LC)
- Gout (LC)
- Headache (due to infection but indicated for tension headaches)
- Heart Attack
- Hematoma (LC)
- Hemophilia
- hepatitis (for acute hepatitis)
- Hernia (LC)
- Herpes simplex (LC)
- Herpes zoster
- Hives (in acute stages)
- Inflammation (acute inflammation) but may be okay or subacute situations
- Interstitial cystitis (LC)
- Jaundice
- Kidney stones
- Lice and Mites
- Enlarged Liver
- Lung Cancer
- Lupus (when having acute flares and may be beneficial in subacute stages) ask Dr.
- Lyme Disease (in the acute stages)
- Lymphangitis
- Marfan's Syndrome (get physicians clearance before any massage)
- Menigitis
- Myositis Ossificans (LC)
- Neuritis (LC)
- Open Wounds/Sores (LC)
- Osteoarthritis (LC)
- Osteogenesis Imperfecti
- Ovarian cysts (LC)
- Paget's Disease
- Pelvic inflammatory disease
- Peripheral neuropathy (LC)
- Peritonitis
- Psoriasis (LC) in acute stages
- Pyelonephritis
- Renal Failure
- Rheumatoid Arthritis (during acute stages)

- Scar Tissue (LC)
- Septic Arthritis
- Sinusitis (for acute infections)
- Spasms (LC) but indicated
- Tendinitis (LC) for acute tendinitis
- Tenosynovitis (LC) in acute stages, indicated in subacute stage
- Thrombophlebitis
- Trigeminal Neuralgia (LC) in acute stage
- Torticollis (under physicians supervision)
- Tuberculosis (when active) with no infection it is okay under supervision of physician
- Ulcerative Colitis (LC) for acute stage
- Ulcers (LC)
- Urinary Tract infection (only massage when in the subacute stage)
- Varicose veins (LC) for extreme veins
- Warts (LC) remember it is possible to get warts from other people. It's a virus.
- Whiplash (in acute stages)   Indicated for subacute stage

When a name appears and has no Local Contraindication, (LC) or anything by that name it is contraindicated (Always check with a physician on any condition in question)

1. If you have a client who sneezes often during the massage and they blow their nose into a tissue and toss it into the waste basket before leaving the treatment room and they have not washed their hands prior to opening the door, what sanitary procedure would you need to do before the next client's appointment?

    You should disinfect the door knob first, and any other objects the client may have touched in the room.   Door knobs carry more germs than any other object in the room.   Always make sure you have a fresh face cover in the face cradle and it would be an excellent idea to disinfect the cradle before and after each client.

2. True or False?   It is never a good idea to work in a dark room.

    True

3. What are some of the symptoms that are associated with having a panic attack?

    a)Shortness of breath, b) Chest pain and c) Increase in heart rate

4. True or False.   If you have extended compression of the radial nerve, this can often result in radial nerve palsy.   **True**

5. Yes or No. Can aluminum poisoning contribute to a possible cause for getting Alzheimer's disease?

    Yes

6. Can pancreatitis be a symptom of irritable bowel syndrome? **No**

7. List at least three symptoms of rheumatoid arthritis.

    Ulnar deviation deformity, morning stiffness, bilateral joint pain in your feet and hand

8. What location does Gout most commonly occur?

    At the first metatarsophalangeal joint

9. The xiphoid process is inferior to the _____. **Sternum**

10. Define srota. **They are channels or pores according to Ayurvedic Theory. (See www.google.com) and type in   Definition of Srota.**

11. What is the main spinal channel in Ayurvedic medicine? **Sushumna nadi**

12. Define nadi. **They are the channels or pathways of energy where prana (ki) flows. This term is used in Ayurvedic medicine.**

13. We have listed this question in a different way as it has been on the Nat'l exam and is worded differently from time to time. Question: Shiatsu is derived from _____ Japanese form of massage? **Anma**

14. The water element consists of what yang organ in the five element theory?

    The Bladder

15. What does Tao mean?

    The law of the universe.

16. Acupressure points are also known as_____? **Tsubos**

17. Which of the following is referred to as the foundation of yin and yang in the body?

    a) **kidney** correct

    b) heart

    c) stomach

    d) other

18.   What is the Five Element Theory?

Five Element Theory is one of the major systems of thought within traditional Chinese medicine. Also referred to as the "five phase" theory by some practitioners, Five Element theory has been used for more than 2,000 years as a method of diagnosis and treatment. While it is an important component of traditional Chinese medicine, today Five Element theory is not used by every acupuncturist and doctor of Oriental medicine; rather, it is employed to a certain degree, depending on the practitioner's training and education, and the style of acupuncture that he or she practices.

19.   In the five element theory, the _____element consists of muscles.
       Earth element

20.   True or False. In the five element theory, the spiritual aspect of water is the will.   **True**

21.   True of False. In the five element theory the water element consists of the bladder, a yang organ.
       True

22.   Is the stomach associated with the earth element and referred to as a yang organ?   **Yes**

23.   What is located at the base of the spine and is referred to as muladhara?
       The root chakra

24.   True or False. The governing vessel regulates all of the yin channels.   **True**

25.   What do chakras do?   **Control the flow of prana/energy.**

26.   What element does the heart meridian and small intestine meridian belong to?
       The fire element

27.   What element does the triple heater meridian belong to?   **The fire element**

28.   Where is the Great Eliminator (a tsubo) located?
       Between the thumb and the forefinger

29.   Define pitta.
       It is the digestion of food and metabolism of the body and is referred to as 'pitta dosha.'

30.   What is a dosha?

It is your Ayurveda mind and body type. There are three doshas. Vata, pitta, and kapha

31.   Where do you apply moxibustion?

Over the acupuncture points

32.   Name some of the functions of the pitta dosha.

Responsible for Digestion conversions, maintains body temperature and hormonal levels, and provides heat and energy to the body, and it sharpens intellect and memory, provides color, odor, texture and luster to the skin.

33.   What is moxibustion?

It is a method of heating by using an herb, artemesia vulgaris.

34.   What gland is the heart charka associated with?

The thymus gland.

35.   Name the seven charkas.

Crown, third eye (brow), throat, heart, solar plexus, hara, and root.

36.   In Sports Massage, Overload is defined as what?

a) making the body work harder than normal   b) carrying too much weight than is necessary for the exercise   c) Over training   d) Making the body work harder than it is accustomed to working

37.   How would you define resistive movement?

Client resists the therapist's movements at the joint, or therapist's resists clients movement.

38.   Muscle fatigue is defined as an inability of a muscle to what?   **Sustain contraction**

39.   What is known as yang or hollow organ?   **The stomach**

40.   Where is the gallbladder meridian located?

It is partially located on the lateral aspect of the hip, leg and foot.

41.   Oriental Medicine treats the _____.   **Cause**

42.   Tsubos are also known as _____.   **Trigger Points**

43.   It is the _____vessel that is a reservoir of yang energy.   **Governing**

44.   It is the _____vessel that is a reservoir of yin energy.   **Conception**

45.   What is the primary meridian in the back?   **The bladder meridian**

46.   Abduction of the thigh is an action of what muscles?
       Gluteus medius and minimus, and the obturator internus

47.   What nerve is the gluteus maximus innervated by?   **Inferior gluteal**

48.   The _____ _____ is the most lateral muscle closest to the mastoid of the
       suboccipital triangle.
       Splenius Capitis

49.   What percentage of disease are caused by stress?   **75%**

50.   If a client arrives for a treatment and has a post operative scar, how long after
       the operation can you perform a massage?   **6 months**

51.   When massaging the quadriceps which muscle is the most exterior to the outer
       thigh?
       The vastus lateralis

52.   If a client has very tight gastrocnemuis they may do what?
       Wear high heel shoes frequently

53.   If your client is in a prone position with a support under the abdomen, the
       support is used for?
       Raising the back allowing the back to be massaged more easily

54.   A client has stiff calf muscles. What would you work on?
       Gastrocnemius

55.   What is the largest organ you can massage?   **The Skin**

56.   How long do you need to be in employment before you are entitled to
       maternity pay?   **26 weeks**

57.   How long do you have to be in employment before you can get a 'contract for employment?'

Two months

58.   How often should an electrical inspection take place?

At least once a year.

59.   What should a 'dry' fire extinguisher not be used for?   **Fat Pan**

60.   What would be the most expensive in advertising (TV/radio, newspaper, word of mouth, flyer drop)?   **TV/Radio**

61.   How would you treat someone who has just fainted suffering from an electric shock?

62.   What would you use a UV cabinet for?   **For storage of pre sterilized equipment.**

63.   True or False. Autoclave will sterilize equipment.

The below was sent in to our company on May 11ᵗʰ and the student had just taken the exam.   Here are some of the things she said were on the exam. We are sending the book out on the 15ᵗʰ for printing so you may have to research some of the below answers between number 63. and 64.

Business Studies:

In cash accounting what VAT payments do you make?

Question on Sole trading Question of Limited Company Question on Partnerships.

Question on Variable costs.

Question on Data Protection

What is Carbon Dioxide extinguisher used for?   a) Electrical b) water c) paper d)?

What is the VAT rate? a)12% b)15% c)17.5% d) 20%

What is NOT required on products? a)country where made b) color c) ingredients d)volume of container

Question on Code of Ethics

What would you do if a client arrived with a medical oedema?

Massage Theory:

Client arrives who has had major back surgery, can you treat:

a) with gentle massage   b) with gentle massage after 1 month   c) after 2 years   d) after 5 years

What technique is known to 'encourage healing and better health through better posture'?

a) Bowen b) homeopathy c) Alexander d) Bach

What treatment uses feet as maps of body?   **Reflexology**

What technique would you use if a client presents with tension in the Tibialis Anterior?

a) tapotement   b) pettrissage   c) effleurage   d) cupping

1. Your massage client was involved in an auto accident and is anxious to settle the case. Your client tells you they would like to continue receiving sessions following the settlement. Should you:

    a. Make up bills for services not yet provided for them to submit to insurance

    b. Call your client's claim adjustor to let them know what your client would like to do so your fees may be included in the case

    c. Immediately contact the authorities and turn your client in for fraud

    d. Ask your client to contact their attorney so that the attorney can negotiate your fees in the settlement

2. Your client asks you to change modalities in mid session. You should:

    a. Tell your client you will, but continue as before

    b. Tell your client you cannot do that, but will be happy to use a different modality next time

    c. Accommodate your client's request

3. There was a question about the client coming in with a migraine in process. What type of work would you perform? **The answers included: tapping on the areas where the migraine hurt the worst and massaging the muscles along either side of the cervical vertebrae.**

4. Which skin condition is contagious? The answer from the choices given was: **Impetigo.**

5. There were two questions about proper body mechanics. The choices of answers were:

    a. For endurance and balance and

    b. To prevent injury to the massage therapist

6. The pyloric valve is between which two organs? **Stomach and small intestine (duodenum)**

7. Why is diaper draping effective? **The genitals can be discretely covered and at the same time the massage therapist is able to see and work other parts of the body.**

8. There was a question where the client has flat feet and is complaining about pain on the bottom of the foot. Which two muscles would you be sure to work? **Answers included: flexor and extensor digitorum, extensor digitorum and peroneus tertius, and peroneus longus.**

9.   Blood moves into the right ventricle during: Some of the choices were:

     a.   Diastolic

     b.   Systolic

     c.   Oxytocin

10.   Hyperflexion of the neck affects which muscles?

     a.   Anterior neck muscles

     b.   Posterior neck muscles

     c.   Hyoid

     d.   Suprahyoid

11.   The most common reason the body moves into flexion and forward motion is due to:

     3 of the several choices:

     a.   Gravity

     b.   Insomnia

     c.   Exercise

12.   Muscular dystrophy is a degeneration of muscle fibers leading to:

Answer was: atrophy in the skeletal muscles

13.   There was also another question about muscular dystrophy and specifically where the degeneration occurs. Two of the several choices included were: (a) the body of the muscle and (b) other

14.   Children who don't receive touch in the early stages of their development often have: two of the several choices:

     a.   Postural and muscular deficiencies

     b.   Increased sensory input

     c.   Decreased motor skills

16.   There was a question which was couched as the definition of osteoarthritis.

The best exercise for osteoporosis is: swimming was one of the several choices

17.   There was a question which was couched as the definition of referred pain.

     In evaluating a client with lordosis, you can expect to see:

     some of the several choices were:

     a.   Anterior pelvic tilt

     b.   Posterior

18.   What is the most important of the endocrine glands? **The answer was: the pituitary [it regulates and controls the activities of other endocrine glands and many body processes]**

THE IMPORTANCE OF MEDICAL HISTORY FORMS

It is very important for you to have a client fill out a Medical Intake Form. When you go to a physician's office for the first time you are required to fill out a Medical History Form.

It is just as important for you to have a prospective client fill out a form before you determine if they should have a massage.

Did you know there are over 80 contraindications for massage therapy and Bodywork? There are many you should be aware of. They are listed in this book.   I have provided a sample form for you following this information. There are many reasons for having a prospective client fill out the intake form, and to interview your client to determine their needs, expectations, as well as setting your own policies and boundaries.

Some of the reasons are:

- you need to explain the procedures after you have reviewed the intake form

- you need to ask specific/pertinent questions

- you need to listen to your clients responses

- determine the type of treatment

- be professional, courteous as well as sensitive

- be specific about the kind of therapy/treatment

- ask what you client expects from the treatment/s

- be prepared to answer questions about your training, credentials and treatments

- you provide and the expected results

- remember to start all of your sessions with questions to determine   any changes that may have occurred since their last treatment

- sexual boundaries should be clearly stated

- professional fees should be stated prior to any treatments

- clearly state what your policy is for i.e. canceled and/or late appointments

[SAMPLE]   MASSAGE THERAPY AND BODYWORK INTAKE FORM

Name_____

Date_____

Address_____Telephone_____

City/State/Zip_____Business _____

Occupation_____ SS#_____

Male_____ Female_____

Is Mother living? _____ Is Father living?_____

How did you find out about my service? _____

Was there a specific reason for seeking massage
therapy?_____

Have you have massage treatments before?_____

If so, by whom?_____

What is your reason for desiring massage treatments? _____

Were you referred by someone?_____

By whom?_____

How would you describe you describe your general health?_____

Are you currently under a health care professional/s? _____ If so, please list them.

Name_____Name_____

Phone Numbers:_____ _____

Are you currently taking any medication? _____If so, list all medications including
hormone replacement therapy, Aspirin, Advil, herbs, and any over the counter pills,
etc. _____

_____

May I have permission to contact your health care professional/s, therapist/s for
further evaluation? _____

Have you had any serious operations, traumatic accidents, chronic illness, chronic
pain, chronic virus infections, and have you been under the care of a psychotherapist,
psychiatrist, counselor, in the past twelve
months?_____   If so, please be specific._____

_____

Has there been any history of the following in your family?

Heart problems_____If so, who?_____

Diabetes _____If so, who?_____

High blood pressure _____If so, who?_____

Low blood pressure _____ If so, who?_____

Arthritis _____ If so, who?_____

Depression _____ If so, who?_____

Cancer _____ If so, who?_____

Have you ever been tested for HIV and if so when? _____

In case of an emergency who would I notify?

Name_____ Phone No/s: (   ) _____

Address_____   Phone No/s: (   ) _____

City/State/Zip_____

Have you had any of the following within the past three to four months? There are
contraindications for these maladies.   Please place a check by each one that would
apply: LC beside a condition would indicate (Locally contraindicated)

____ Abortion (no deep abdominal work)

____ Aneurysm (not even if you suspect a client who fits the profile for aneurysms)

____ Appendicitis, however after appendicitis operation it can be beneficial with Dr's
permission

____ Acne (LC, you don't want to spread the infection)

____ Advanced atherosclerosis

____ Baker's cysts (LC)

_____ Boils (LC)
_____ Bronchitis (LC)
_____ Bunions (LC)
_____ Burns (LC)
_____ Bursitis(LC)
_____ Cancer (should be done only with physicians approval)
_____ Candidiasis (LC)
_____ Cirrhosis (LC in advanced stages)
_____ Crohn's disease: (LC, some massage with physicians supervision)
_____ Cysts (LC)
_____ Dermatitis (LC)
_____ Ovarian cysts (LC)
_____ Paget's Disease
_____ Pelvic inflammatory disease
_____ Peripheral neuropathy (LC)
_____ Peritonitis
_____ Psoriasis (LC) in acute stages
_____ Pyelonephritis
_____ Renal Failure
_____ Rheumatoid Arthritis (during acute stages)
_____ Scar Tissue (LC)
_____ Septic Arthritis
_____ Sinusitis (for acute infections)
_____ Spasms (LC) but indicated
_____ Tendinitis (LC) for acute tendinitis
_____ Tenosynovitis (LC) in acute stages, indicated in subacute stage
_____ Thrombophlebitis
_____ Trigeminal Neuralgia (LC) in acute stage
_____ Torticollis (under physician's supervision)
_____ Tuberculosis (when active) with no infection it is okay under supervision of physician
_____ Ulcerative Colitis (LC) for acute stage
_____ Ulcers (LC)
_____ Urinary Tract infection (only massage when in the subacute stage)
_____ Varicose veins (LC) for extreme veins
_____ Warts (LC) remember it is possible to get warts from other people. It's a virus.
_____ Whiplash (in acute stages)   Indicated for subacute stage

When a name appears and has no (Local Contraindication, LC) or anything by that name it is contraindicated (Always check with a physician on any condition in question)

~

I have filled out the Intake Form to be best of my ability and understand that massage therapy treatments are not meant to replace a Doctor's treatment. I also understand that massage and bodywork treatments are considered to be an additional aid in the helping me to improve and/or maintain a healthy body. I have been told by the therapist that all information discussed during treatments is to remain confidential. I also understand if I fail to cancel any appointments 24 hours prior to a scheduled appointment, I will be responsible for paying the full fee. If an emergency prevents my calling to cancel I understand I will not be charged.

Signature_____
Date_____

THIS IS JUST A SAMPLE FORM AND YOU MAY WANT TO IMPROVISE

SECTION III

QUESTIONS AND ANSWERS FROM PREVIOUS 2005 AND 2006 EDITIONS.

THROUGHOUT THIS ENTIRE BOOK THERE MAY BE QUESTIONS THAT HAVE NOT ANSWERS. YOU CAN FIND ALL ANSWERS BY SEARCHING ON THE INTERNET UNDER WWW.GOOGLE.COM

1.   In reflexology treatments, what area on the foot would have the pressure point relating to the neck in treatment?   **big toe, base of big toe.**

2.   In massage treatment is it a general practice to massage by muscle groups? **Yes**

3.   Is the back effleuraged before petrissage movement? **Yes**

4.   Should you always be in a standing position while massaging a patient?   No

5.   What is Aroma Therapy?

      Various scents which are added to massage lubricants or used in a vapor type of machine, which has either a stimulating or relaxing effect

6.   What are meridians and how many regular meridians are there?

      Oriental philosophy/medical science believe that meridians are a system of pathways or channels pertaining to energy (ki) that circulates in a network of channels and collateral in the body. There are 12 regular or main meridians.

7.   Name at least 4 benefits of good posture.

      Improves circulation, appearance, prevents fatigue and backaches, and better on your muscles and joints

8.   Where did Yoga originate?   **India**

9.   It is important to exercise when dieting for weight loss, and if so give the reason why?

      Yes, because it firms as well as proportions the body as it burns calories

10.   What is one of the most popular forms of exercise and list at least 2 benefits?

      Walking, because there is no equipment required. It improves your circulation.

11. What is TMJ dysfunction and how can you treat it?

TMJ is temporomandibular joint. The mandibular, which plays an important role in jaw pain, has muscles that are attached to the mandibular and if there are spasms in this area the jaw point (in pressure point therapy) can well respond to pressure.

12. What is torticollis? **Latin term for twisted neck. (tortus) twisted and (collis) neck**

13. What are some of the benefits of lymphatic massage/drainage?

Purifies and regenerates tissues, expedites the balance of the body's internal chemistry, helps to balance the functions of all body organs as well as the immune system

14. True or False. Damaged tissue can be carried away during massage, and circulation of blood enables the nutrients to enter the damaged area helping the healing process. **True**

15. What role do the liver, pancreas, and glands in the small intestine play in the digestion process?

They supply digestive secretions

16. Define pathogenic. **It is harmful bacteria**

17. What is the longest muscle in the body, and where is it located?

Sartorius -located in the leg (thigh)

18. Give the definition of a bone.

A bone is a form of dense connective tissue which supports the muscles of the body and protects delicate internal structures, and produces blood cells

19. What is Reflexology?

Reflexology is the application of applying pressure to a reflex point (usually on the hands and feet) to relieve tension and, improve blood supply to certain regions of the body to help normalize body functions.

20. What do enzymes do?

Aid in digestion

21. Name some of the benefits of a facial massage.

Helps to keep the muscles toned, increases circulation of blood, and keeps the oil and sweat glands functioning properly.

22. Describe what a centripetal movement is.

A centripetal movement is a strong pressure directed towards a center i.e. the heart and it follows the direction of the blood current

23. True or False. Light rays are very beneficial in the treatment of varicose veins. **False**

24. Define ligament. **Connective tissue connecting bones to bones**

25. True or False. Diastolic is a higher reading than systolic. **False**

26. Name at least 4 ethical codes pertaining to massage therapy.

(1) have a good understand of massage

(2) keep your appointments

(3) do not take advantage of a client

(4) explain the draping to the client before the massage

27. Name the 3 arches in the foot. **Transverse, medial longitudinal, and lateral**

28. What is a catheter? **A tube for fluids**

29. What are the 4 basic movements used in massage therapy and name the various forms/names of these movements?

(1) Percussion =slapping , tapping, cupping, hacking beating

(2) Compression = petrissage /friction/vibration

(3) Joint = passive and active movements

(4) Effleurage = stroking with palm of hand or fingertips   Note: Tapotement is also referred to as a tapping movement

30. Describe what a "passive movement" means in massage.

It is when the joints are massaged and the client does not have to actively move their muscles

31. In massage therapy, what is the meaning of "contraindication"?

It would not be advisable to massage because of the client's condition and massage might be harmful more than helpful

32. Name 3 forms of harmful bacteria. **Spirilla, bacilli and cocci**

33. What is Shiatsu?   **Shiatsu is a treatment whereby you apply pressure with the ball of your thumb along the meridians to increase circulation.**

34. What is Zygote?   **What is the zygomatic process? Zygote is fertilized ovum. Zygomatic process is the process of the temporal or squamosal bone helping to form the zygomatic arch.**

35. What are the gonads?   **Sex glands (the ovaries and testes)**

36. Name the 3 separate bones of the hip bone.   **Ilium, ischium, and pubis**

37. True or False. The brain is the vital force which controls all the body functions. **True**

38. Name the four general classifications of bones and give one example of each.

     Long = femur, short = ankle, irregular = vertebrae, and flat= scapula

39. True or False. The nerves are the vital force that activates all muscle functions. **True**

40. Give the basic principles for draping a client.

     Any tight clothing should be removed first of all, and either a towel or sheet should be used to cover the parts of the body that are not being massaged. It is important to make sure that the client is not embarrassed or exposed unnecessarily. The purpose is for the client to be comfortable, relaxed and at ease. All of your movements should be very businesslike.

41. Please be specific in describing how you would drape a female client using the "top cover method".

     When the client is on the table have the top cover (can be either a large sheet, or large bath towel), cover the client lengthwise covering the entire body all but the head. When you massage the arm you would fold the top cover exposing only the area that you are massaging.   When you massage the leg, you would tuck the cover under the opposite leg positioning the cover tightly (but not too tight) along the inguinal crease

42. Describe the diaper draping method in detail.

     You would use a very large towel (terry towel preferably) for covering the chest and long enough to come to a little bit above the knees of the client. You would then fold the end of the towel (end just above the knees) into four smooth folds. These folds taper to fit the contours of the body. The clients leg would then be raised enough to allow the end of the towel to be tucked under the sacrum. The client is then draped properly.

43. Describe in detail how you would drape a female client properly before you would begin an abdominal massage.

You would fold another towel (in additional to the one covering the body) to cover the breasts and place it over the first towel. Then you would pull the first towel down while you hold the folded towel and place it over the breasts. Then you would take the original first cover of the client and fold the top of this first towel across the client's pelvic area. Then you would raise the client's arm and then tuck the towel (the folded one for the breasts) and tuck this securely under the scapula. Then you would put the client's arm down and follow the same procedure for the other arm, etc.

44. How are cold applications beneficial?

Stimulates the nerves - increases movement of body cells - improves your circulation

45. Name one benefit of a hot water treatment.

Increases circulation of blood to the surface of the skin

46. Name the organs of the respiratory system.

Lungs, bronchial tubes, trachea, nose, and mouth

47. What is another name for the trachea?   **Windpipe**

48. What is Fascia?

A tough connective tissue that has an elastic component and a matrix that is a gelatinous like substance

49. What is Myofascial Release?

A hands-on technique that applies prolonged light pressure with specific directions into the fascia system

50. How many bones are found in the upper leg and give the names of these bones?

One. The Femur

51. Is it really necessary to get a medical record of a client?   **Yes**

52. In Sports/Athletic massage, what are the major applications?

Massage before, during and after an event and also during any rehabilitation

53.   What are the connecting links between arteries and veins called?   **Capillaries**

54.   Name the five divisions of the spine.

Cervical vertebrae, thoracic vertebrae, lumbar vertebrae, sacrum vertebrae, and the coccygeal vertebrae (also called the coccyx)

55.   Define what muscle tone is.

When muscle fibers are constantly in a state of slight contraction

56.   What part of the body is the Achilles Tendon located?   **Just above the heel**

57.   List at least 3 things a massage therapist should do in order to maintain hygiene and sanitation.

(1) wash hands before and after each treatment

(2) keep nails short and trimmed so that you won't scratch a client

(3) have clean sheets, linens, and towels available for each client, and change linens after each treatment

58.   Define tissue.   **A group or collection of cells which act together in the performance of a particular function**

59.   Define Anatomy.   **Anatomy is the study of the structure of the body.**

60.   Define Physiology?   **Physiology is the study of the functions of the body.**

61.   Where does the digestion of proteins begin turning into amino acids?   **In the stomach**

62.   Describe what "active movement" is in massage therapy.

The client participates in the exercises in which the voluntary muscles are contracted.

63.   What is Acupuncture and what is an integral part of this type of treatment?

Acupuncture is a treatment where the skin is punctured with needles along certain meridians of the body for therapeutic purposes.

64.   Name at least 14 other body therapies or specialized massage techniques other than Swedish massage therapy.   **Rolfing, Feldenkrais, Myofascial Release, Reiki, Trager, Shiatsu, Deep Tissue Technique (Athletic/Sports), Reflexology, Lymphatic Drainage, Structural Integration, Polarity, Acupressure, Cranial Sacral Therapy, Jin Shin Do.**

65.   What is hydrotherapy?   **Water treatments for the external part of the body**

66.   When are salt rubs given?   **Anytime or following a cabinet bath or hot bath**

67.   How high can a temperature be in a steam vapor?   **140 degrees Fahrenheit**

68.   True or False. The skin can safely tolerate 120 degrees Fahrenheit.
       FALSE. 110 degrees Fahrenheit

69.   Name at least 10 parts of the body involved in the process of digestion.
       Teeth, tongue, salivary glands, mouth, stomach, liver, gallbladder, pancreas, small intestine and gastric glands

70.   Name a couple of contraindications in Sports/Athletic massage.
       Injury, illness or any abnormal condition

71.   Name the various massage movements that have a stimulating effect on the nervous system.
       Vibration, friction, and percussive movements

72.   What can Structural Integration do?   **It can endeavor to bring the physical composition of the body into alignment and balance around a central axis**

73.   Can massage relieve anxiety?   **Yes**

74.   What muscles can cross both the hip and the knee and act on both joints?
       The hamstrings

75.   Name 4 gastrointestinal disorders.
       Constipation - Ulcers - Spastic colon - Irritable bowel syndrome

76.   What is impetigo?   **A skin infection that could be caused by strep or staph**

77.   What is reflexology?   **It is the application of applying pressure to a reflex point (usually on the hands, feet) to relieve tension, improve the blood supply to certain regions of the body to help normalize body functions.**

78.   What is Rolfing and what is one benefit of having Rolfing treatments?
       Rolfing is a method of structural integration, and a deep connective tissue massage. One benefit is that it increases suppleness of the muscles.

79. True or False. Nonpathogenic bacteria are also harmful.

   False: sometimes they are helpful

80. What function does the diaphragm perform?

   Aids in the expansion and contraction of the lungs

81. Why should the massage therapist explain the draping technique to their client?

   It prevents embarrassment to the client as well as the therapist.

82. In what part of the body are starches digested into the sugar stage? **The mouth and small intestine**

83. What are some of the things that can be relieved by applying shiatsu?

   Insomnia, high blood pressure, headaches, nervous tension, sore muscles, constipation.

84. What does Shiatsu mean?

   Pressure of the finger - broken down it means (finger/shi) (atsu/ pressure)

85. In sports/athletic massage what are the goals of the pre-event massage and the goals for the post-event massage?

   Goal for the pre-event massage is to increase the flexibility and circulation in the areas of the body that are going to be used; the goal in the post-event massage is to increase the circulation in order to clear out the metabolic wastes, to quiet the nervous system and to reduce any muscle spasms and/or tension

86. Describe what a Centrifugal movement is.

   A movement away from the center causing a decrease in the flow of blood lessening pressure to the heart

87. In heat and lamp treatments what are the 3 rays used?

   Ultraviolet, visible light and infrared

88. Name one thing that is very important for the massage therapist to do in order to avoid fatigue and backache during treatment?

   Pay attention to good posture and make sure that the massage table is at the proper level for the therapists height

89. True or False. One of the benefits of a whirlpool bath is a decrease in blood circulation.

   False - there is an increase

90.   What is a pore, sometimes referred to as a follicle?
A minute opening of the sweat glands on the surface of the skin

91.   What are the 2 types of bone tissue? **Compact and spongy**

92.   True or False. Bones receive nourishment through blood vessels that enter through the periosteum into the interior of the bone.   **True**

93.   True or False. A lesion is a structural change in the tissue and can be caused by either injury or disease.   **True**

94.   Can massage relieve anxiety?   **Yes**

95.   What percentage of an adult's body weight is skeletal muscle?   **40%**

96.   What 3 main techniques are used in acupressure?
Pressing the pressure points, touching and rubbing these pressure points

97.   Where did acupuncture originate?   **China**

98.   What is the main cause of foot problems today?
Wearing shoes that are not fitted properly

99.   Sports massage is also referred to what other name?   **Athletic Massage**

100.   Name a massage movement/technique that has a calming effect on the nervous system.
Petrissage - light effleurage or a very gentle stroking and light friction

101.   What should the temperature be in your massage therapy room?
75 to 80 degrees F.

102.   What is lymphangiitis?   **Blood poisoning or inflammation of the lymphatic vessels**

103.   Define Pathology.   **The part of medicine that is concerned with the structural and functional changes caused by disease**

104.   Name the 3 sections of the spine.   **Cervical - Thoracic - Lumbar**

105.   Name 3 skeletal dysfunctions.

Lordosis (swayback) - Scoliosis (an abnormality of the spine with pain) - Kyphosis (humpback)

106.   What lubricates the joints?   **Synovial fluid**

107.   What purpose does cartilage and ligaments serve?

List the purpose of cartilage first. Cartilage cushions the bones at joints i.e. preventing jarring between bones, and gives shape to the external features on the body i.e. your ear and nose. Ligaments help support bones at the joints i.e. the wrist.

108.   What is fossa?   **A depression**

109.   What is sebum?   **The oily secretion/substance that comes from the sebaceous gland**

110.   What is sinus?   **A cavity within a bone**

111.   Name one function of bone marrow.

Bone marrow helps in the nutrition of the bone

112.   True or False. A very effective way to bring blood to an area is through the application of ice.   **False, it restricts blood flow to the area**

113.   Define a duct.   **A canal for fluids**

114.   What are the appendages of the skin?

Nails -hair and also the sweat/oil glands

115.   Name a joint that is immovable.   **Synarthrotic**

116.   How would you massage over the bones?

You would follow the form of the bones very carefully

117.   What muscle opens the eye?

The levator palpebrae superioris muscle

118.   What are the 10 most important systems of the body?

Nervous - skeletal - respiratory - reproductive - digestive - circulatory - muscular - endocrine - integumentary and excretory system

119.   The urinary system is part of what system?
Excretory system

120.   The blood vascular and lymph vascular is part of what system?
Circulatory system

121.   What is a clear, yellow fluid that bathes cells?   **Interstitial fluid associated with lymph**

122.   What are the 4 main anatomic parts of the body?
The extremities, trunk, spine and head

123.   What does integument mean?   **Skin or covering**

124.   A patient comes to you and had just sprained their ankle. There is considerable swelling and a lot of pain. What type of treatment would you give?
Massage above and below the area in an attempt to reduce the swelling and help alleviate the pain.

125.   A 65 year old woman has had arthritis of the spine for several years and she stands in a slightly flexed position. When she tries to stand in a normal position there is a lot of pain. What type of treatment would you give?
Massage to relieve pain and any spasms and also heat

126.   A court reporter is recovering from surgery for Carpal Tunnel Syndrome. Her left hand is very painful. The finger flexors are stiff and she is having a very hard time using her hand. What type of treatment would you give?
Exercise to assist her in regaining use of her hand, massage, and heat treatments

127.   What is meant by reflex effects?
When your hands stimulate the sensory receptors of the skin and subcutaneous tissues it causes reflex effects. Example: Lymphatic flow is an effect of deep pressure treatments by stroking or compression movements.

128   What is meant by venostasis (syn: phlebostasis) and list three contraindications when you would not massage situations showing venostasis?
It is a condition that develops due to muscular inactivity whereby gravity inhibits the normal venous return towards the heart. You would not massage if there is a possibility of spreading inflammation,

possibility of dislodging a thrombus, or if there is this type of obstruction that the assistance of massage would not improve the venous flow.

129   How do muscles maintain a metabolic balance?

Usually through normal activity...when they contract they get rid of toxic products

130.   Define edema and 3-4 causes of edema.

Edema is excess interstitial fluid in the tissues, aka swelling.

(1) increased resistance to outflow at the venous end of the capillary bed, (2) decreased resistance to flow through the arterioles and capillary sphincters that supply the capillary bed, and (3) increased gravitational forces.

131.   Will massage reduce obesity?   **No**

132.   Can massage take the place of active exercise.   **No**

133.   What is a hematoma?   **A swelling that contains blood**

134.   How many ribs are there in the body?   **24**

135.   Define condyle.

A rounded knuckle, or articular surface like prominence usually at a point of articulation or at the extremity of a bone

136.   What are bursae?

Little sacks lined with synovial membrane and lubricated with synovial fluid

137   Name the movements of the diarthrotic joints.

Gliding, pivoting, saddle, ball and socket, hinge movements

138   Internal rotation means to move where?   **Medially or toward the midline**

139.   External rotation means to move where?   **Laterally or away from midline**

140.   Hyperextension movement means what?

To increase the angle beyond the anatomical position

141   What does flexion mean?   **To decrease the angle at a joint**

142.   What does extension mean? **To increase the angle at a joint**

143.   What does circumduction mean? **To move the distal end of an extremity in a circle while the proximal end remains fixed**

144   What does adduction mean? **To move a part toward the midline**

145.   What does dorsiflexion mean? **To move the foot upward**

146.   What does plantar flexion mean? **To move the foot downward (to extend downward)**

147.   What does inversion mean? **To turn the plantar surface toward the midline**

148.   What does eversion mean? **To turn the plantar surface away from the midline**

149.   What does pronation mean? **To move the palm downward**

150.   What does protraction mean? **To move a part of the body forward**

151.   What does depression (in movement) mean? **To lower a part of the body**

152.   What is fibromylasia?

A disorder - the musculoskeletal function throwing the neurovascular system "off balance". Many factors that can precipitate it are personality, disordered sleep patterns, occupation, hobbies, posture, weather, etc.

153.   What is the difference between asthma and bronchitis?

Asthma is a panting - paroxysmal dyspnea accompanied by the adventitious sounds caused by a spasm of the bronchial tubes or due to swelling of their mucous membrane. Bronchitis is the inflammation of bronchial mucous membranes.

154.   What is the difference between neuralgia and neuritis?

Neuralgia is acute pain extending along the course of one or more nerves, and neuritis is inflammation of a nerve/s usually associated with a degenerative process.

155.   What causes a duodenal ulcer? **Action of gastric juices**

156. What is colitis/spastic colon?

It is inflammation of the colon, attacks occur spasmodically accompanied by constipation. Spastic, colicky pain in mid-abdomen. Tenacious, gelatinous mucus and shreds of mucous membrane may be passed.

157. What are some of the things that you want to ask in your interviewing a new patient?

Did a physician suggest treatments, have you had any injuries, accidents, etc. and be sure and cover all things that may be a contraindication to treatment before you start a massage. Take temperature before treatment, and ask for a complete medical history so you will know if there is high blood pressure, ulcers, etc.

158. Define what is the origin of a muscle and what is the insertion of a muscle.

The more proximal attachment site of a muscle is referred to as the origin, and the more distal attachment site of a muscle is called the insertion.

159. Name two endangerment sites on the body.

Popliteal fossa and femoral triangle

160. Why is it important that once you start a treatment that it not be interrupted?

You do not want to interrupt any flow of rhythm or cause the patient to become disturbed in anyway.

161. Name 6 functions of the skin.

Protects the body - regulates the temperature - acts as a excretory and secretory organ - oxygen is taken in and carbon dioxide is discharged through the process called respiration - and -absorption

162. How many bones are in the adult human body and be specific i.e. EXAMPLE: lower extremities (62 bones)?

spine = vertebrae 26 bones, head = face (14) cranium (8) ear (6) hyoid bone (1) 26 bones, thorax = ribs and sternum 25 bones, and the upper extremities 64 bones.

163. What 3 things compose the skeletal system?

Ligaments -bones - cartilage

164. What is the largest organ of the body?

The skin

165.   Name two main layers of the skin.

Dermis & epidermis

166.   What are the layers of the epidermis and the epidermis of the palms and soles?

The mucosum, granulosum, lucidum, and stratum corneum, and the palms and soles have the following strata: stratum corneum, stratum lucidum, stratum granulosum, stratum spinosum), and stratum gasale, and the other parts of the body, the stratum lucidum may be absent in some cases.

167.   What are the 2 major glands in the skin and tell what the function is of these glands?

Sebaceous = Secrete sebum,   and   Sudoriferous = Excretes sweat

168.   What is one of the goals in receiving Rolfing treatments?

To reshape the body's physical posture as well as to realign the muscular and connective tissue.

169.   Name the inorganic matter found in bones.

Calcium carbonate and calcium phosphate

170.   Name the organic matter found in bones.

Marrow - blood vessels - bone cells

171.   What is periosteum?   **It is the protective covering of the bone**

172.   Define joints.   **Joints are the connections between the surfaces of bones.**

173.   How do most massage therapists begin a massage?

Generally with the client in a face up position unless the client prefers the prone position

174.   Name some contraindications in massage.

Abnormal body temperature, infectious disease, varicose veins, phlebitis, aneurosa, high blood pressure, edema, cancer (in extreme conditions recovering from radiation treatment, however; massage is wonderful for cancer patients but should be done by someone who is trained in this area), intoxication, chronic fatigue, psychosis, hernia

175.   Name the 12 cranial nerves.

Olfactory

Hypoglossal

Spinal accessory

Optic

Oculomotor

Facial

Vestibulocochlear

Vagus/pneumogastric

Trochlear

Trigeminal/trifacial

Glossopharyngeal

Abducent

176. What is the first thing that you would do if you suspected a heart attack?
Place the individual in a comfortable position

177. Would you use cold applications in the treatment of tendonitis?   **Yes**

178. Entrapment of the peroneal nerve can result from an improper massage technique on the:
a. forehead,   b. upper arm,   c. front of thigh   **d. back of knee**

179. What are the effects of percussion?
a.   breaks up adhesions and reduces scar tissue
b.   aids in shedding of dead skin cells and reduces blemishes
c.   increases range of motion and strengthens muscle
d.   tones the muscles and stimulates circulation
e.   tones muscles/stimulates circulation

180. Which massage movement is used to break down the adhesions of a well-healed scar?
Friction

181. Which of the following is a bony landmark on the anterior pelvic girdle?
a. Sacrum   b. Greater trochanter   c. Ischial tuberosity   **d. Pubic symphysis**

182. Which of the following is a flexor of the hip?
a. Piriformis
b. Biceps femoris
c. Iliopsoas
d. Gluteus maximus

183.   Define what a Trager session consists of.

Is it a gentle rocking and the movement of muscles, limbs, and joints in order to produce sensory experiences of freedom, ease, and lightness. The therapist uses their hands and mind to communicate a positive experience through the patient's tissue to the central nervous system.

184.   Define Yin/Yang.

Yin/Yang is a Buddhist theory that demonstrates the natural process of continuous change where nothing is of itself, but is seen as aspects of the whole or as two opposites, yet is complementary aspects of existence itself.

185.   How long should you take a hot bath?   **No longer than 20 minutes maximum**

186.   The heart, blood vessels including the arteries, veins, and capillaries are the main part of what?

The blood-vascular system

187.   What is the usual order of massage movements and list these in order?

Begins with arms (if the client prefers) or back otherwise, then front of legs, chest, neck, and abdomen.

188.   What is the name of the main artery of the body?   **Aorta**

189.   Should a client be advised to drink plenty of water after a massage treatment and if so explain why or why not?

Yes, the system needs to be washed out because you have stimulated the flow of blood, and your body needs the water to flush out the toxins.

190.   Name the functions of the following in their order: veins, heart, arteries, and capillaries.

Veins carry impure blood from the capillaries back to the heart; heart function keeps the blood moving through the body; arteries carry purified blood from the heart to the capillaries; and the capillaries bring nourishment to the cells as well as remove waste products.

191.   Plasma, red corpuscles, platelets, and white corpuscles are found where?

In the blood

192.   What artery supplies blood to the chest, arm, and shoulder?   **Axillary artery**

193. What muscle moves the scalp? **Occipito-Frontalis**

194. What does the masseter muscle do? **Raises the lower jaw**

195. What is the principal large artery on the right side of the neck? **Right carotid artery**

196. What is the function of the pulmonary artery?
Divides into left and right branches and takes the blood into the lungs

197. Venous blood is carried through which artery up to the lungs to be oxygenated and purified?
Pulmonary artery

198. There are two sets of nerves that regulate the heartbeat. What are they?
Sympathetic and the vagus nerves

199. Define lacteals. **They carry chyle from the intestine to the thoracic duct.**

200. What is phlebitis? **Inflammation of a vein accompanied by swelling and pain**

201. What is osteoporosis? **A disease in which there is a decrease in bone density**

202. What three groups of muscles make up the hamstrings?
The posterior thigh (the long head of biceps femoris, semi-membranosus, and semi tendinosus)

203. What are the gluteals? **The muscles of the buttocks**

204. Name at lease 6 lubricants that are used in therapy. **Cocoa butter (used on scar tissue), 70% alcohol (good for stump ends), powder, mineral oil/baby oil, lanolin based cold cream, vegetable oil/olive oil (good for baby massage or for anyone that can use the extra nutrients)**

205. What type of treatment would you give to someone who has just had a cast removed after having surgery to relieve recurrent shoulder dislocation?
Tapotement, effleurage, and petrissage to deltoid and trapezius in an attempt to increase the circulation and relieve spasm

206. What type of treatment would you give to a patient who has had severe bursitis in the left shoulder for 2 years? **Heat, massage, and exercise to the left shoulder**

207. For a patient who has severe lower back pain from a herniated disc with severe sciatica associated, and whenever there are any movements from the right leg which stretches the sciatic nerve, it is very painful. What type of treatment would you give? **Petrissage to the lower back area to help relieve the pain however, it might be a good idea to suggest they see a D.O. if they don't already have one.**

208. Tell what the following muscles do:

(a) serratus anterior	**(a) raises ribs in breathing**
(b) obliquus capitis inferior	**(b) rotates cranium**
(c) rectus abdominis	**(c) compresses the abdomen**
(d) trapezius	**(d) draws head backward**
(e) sacrospinalis	**(e) keeps your spine erect**
(f) obliquus capitis superior	**(f) draws head backward**
(g) longus colli	**(g) rotates the spine**
(h) quadratus lumborum	**(h) bends the trunk of body**
(i) latissimus dorsi	**(i) draws arm backward**
(j) sartorius	**(j) rotates thigh outward and leg inward, bends leg/thigh**
(k) pectoralis major	**(k) draws arm forward and downward**
(l) pectoralis minor	**(l) depresses point of shoulder**
(m) intercostales externi	**(m) stretches the chest during breathing**
(n) levatores costarum	**(n) raises the ribs during breathing**
(o) diaphragm	**(o) main muscle of respiration**
(p) temporalis	**(p) raises the lower jaw and presses it against the upper jaw**
(q) recti muscles	**(q) rotates your eyeball**
(r) sternocleidomastoid	**(r) bends your head to one side and forward**
(s) psoas major	**(s) bends trunk on thigh or thigh on trunk**
(t) rhomboid	**(t) draws shoulder blade backward and upward**
(u) infra-spinatus	**(u) rotates arm outwardly**
(v) supra-spinatus	**(v) helps to raise the arm side ward**
(w) deltoid	**(w) extends and bends the arm**
(x) teres minor	**(x) rotates humerus outward**
(y) teres major	**(y) assists in drawing humerus downward and backward**
(z) triceps brachialis	**(z) extends the forearm**

209. What are muscles attached to? **Bones, other muscles, cartilage, ligaments, tendons, skin**

210. What is a characteristic of a amphiarthrotic joint? **It has limited motion.**

211. Define fascia.

Connective tissue covering muscles and separating their layers or groups of layers

212. What is the difference between diarthrotic and synarthrotic joints?

Synarthrotic joints are very limited and diarthrotic joints are freely movable.

213. There are two divisions of the autonomic nervous systems, the sympathetic and the parasympathetic. Which of these expands energy?   **The sympathetic**

214. How many pairs of cranial nerves are there and how many pairs of spinal nerves are there?

12 pairs cranial and 31 pairs spinal

215. The ulnar nerve supplies what two joints?   **Elbow and shoulder joints**

216. The pneumogastric nerve supplies what?   **The heart and lungs, pharynx, esophagus, larynx, stomach, liver and spleen**

217. The greater occipital nerve supplies what?   **The back of the neck**

218. The intercostal nerve supplies what?   **The upper abdomen**

219. What does the sacral nerve supply?   **The muscles and skin of the lower extremities**

220. What nerve supplies the hip and knee joints?   **The obturator nerve**

221. What are hormones?   **The secretions manufactured by the endocrine glands**

222. Where is the pituitary gland located?

Just behind the point of the optic nerve crossing in the brain

223. Name the important endocrine glands.

Pituitary, adrenal, sex glands, thyroid, pancreas

224. What are the two divisions of the vascular system?

Blood vascular system (heart and blood vessels) and the lymph vascular system (lymph glands and lymphatics)

225. Name two diseases of the blood?

hemophilia and anemia

226. The right atrium of the heart receives impure blood from the what?

Vena cava

227. Veins of the abdomen, lower extremities and pelvis empty into what vein?

Inferior vena cava

228. Which ventricle does the aorta send blood to all parts of the body except the lungs?

The left ventricle

229. What is the name of the large artery on the left side of the neck?

The left carotid artery

230. The left atrium receives purified blood through what vein?   **Pulmonary vein**

231. The veins from the neck, head, thorax and upper extremities empty into what vein?

Superior vena cava

232. What does the pulmonary artery do?

It conveys venous blood from the right ventricle to the lungs

233. What is meant by sanitation?   Cleanliness

234. How many bones form the wrist and what are their names?

Eight bones called carpal, scaphoid, lunate, triquetrum, pisiform, trapezium, trapezoid, capitate, and hamate

235. In massage of the lower extremities, the manipulations are applied in what sequence?

Effleurage, tapotement, friction, and nerve strokes

236. Why is massage of the chest muscles beneficial?

Because you are helping the muscles that assist in respiration, and in this way you will be indirectly helping the lungs to perform their

function. It also activates muscles that assist the movements of the arm, as well as that of the shoulders.

237. Why should the client's knees be flexed for abdominal massage?

To relax the abdominal muscles

238. What areas of the body have the thickest skin?

The palms of hands and soles of feet

239. What is a "Charley Horse" and how can it be avoided in applying massage?

It is a spastic muscle contraction and can be avoided by not hacking across the muscle.

240. How much pressure should be applied in friction of the thigh muscles?

Enough pressure to move the underlying muscles

241. How does massage applied to the spinal area improve the bodily functions?

It activates the nerves and brings fresh blood to stimulate and nourish the nerves, which branching out from this area are the means used by the brain to carry messages throughout the body.

242. When pressure is applied on the seventh cranial nerve what muscles are activated?

The facial muscles

243. What is meant by the therapeutic field in hydrotherapy?

Treatment of condition by use of water

244. What is used in a saline bath?   **Common salt**

245. Describe a twisting manipulation that is applied to the muscles?

You place both of your hands next to each other and push the tissue forward with the palm of one hand as the fingers of the other hand pull the tissue back.

246. Define the term "remedial exercises".

It is the application of body movements that maintain or restore normal muscle and joint function.

247. How can the therapist avoid straining a joint?

By knowing the types of movements that each joint is capable of performing

248   Why should the therapist avoid the "hacking" transversely across the muscles?
It could cause a Charley Horse.

249.   Percussion massage is used more on what parts of the body?
Buttocks, thighs, and areas that are heavily muscled

250.   Would you use the hacking motion over the tibia?   No

251.   Name the two movements that the shoulder cannot perform.
Supination and pronation

252.   Explain why you would not want to over stimulate a weak muscle during massage.
It could cause muscle strain and could create some toxic poison.

253.   What is epistaxis?   **A nose bleed**

254.   How do you know if you have used too much oil in a massage treatment?
because your movements will be difficult

255.   What is tonic contraction?
Sustained partial contraction of some of a skeletal muscle in response to stretch receptors is called a tone, or tonic contraction.

256.   What is isotonic? What is isometric contraction?
Isotonic is having the same tension, tone or pressure. Isometric contraction is the contraction of a muscle in which shortening of the muscle is prevented, and tension is developed and does not result in body movement.

257.   True or False. Claustrophobia is a fear of heights.
False.   It is a fear of being confined in a small space.

258.   True or False. Agoraphobia is a dread or fear of crowds of people.   **True**

259.   Give another name for the Lingual Bone.   **Hyoid bone**

260.   What is the difference between peritoneum and periosteum?
Periosteum is the membrane that covers the bones and peritoneum is a closed sac composed of a thin sheet of elastic and fibrous tissue that lines the abdominal cavity.

261. Give the normal body temperature and normal external skin temperature.

Normal body temp. is 98.6 degrees F, and normal external skin temperature is 92 degrees F

262. What is the difference between protoplasm and proprioceptor?

Protoplasm is a jelly like substance within the cell and contains fat, carbohydrates, proteins and mineral salts; and proprioceptor is end organ of a sensory nerve fiber located in muscle and joints .

263. What can friction produce?   **Local hyperemia**

264. True or False. Flexion and extension can be performed as passive Range of Motion on the humeroulnar joint.   **True**

265. Where is the olecranon process found?   **In the proximal ulna**

266. What is a trigger point?

It is a hyper irritable spot that is painful when pressure is applied.

267. When you stimulate an active trigger point what can occur? What do latent trigger points do?

Active trigger points refer pain and tenderness to another part of the body, while latent trigger points exhibit pain when pressure is applied and don't refer pain.

268. Are neuromuscular lesions always hypersensitive to pressure?   **Yes**

269. Neuro-physiological therapies utilize methods of assessing tissues and soft tissue manipulative techniques to do what?

To normalize the tissues and reprogram the neurological loop in order to reduce pain and improve function

270. If your client had arm abduction pain what would be affected?

The deltoid and supraspinatus

271. What are the two basic inhibitory reflexes produced during MET (muscle energy technique) manipulations?

Reciprocal inhibition and isometric relaxation

272. True or False. Isotonic contraction occurs with movement.   **True**

273. What does SMB stand for?   **Structural Muscular Balancing**

274. Define what the following contractions are: Isometric, isotonic, concentric, eccentric.

Isometric muscle contraction is the contraction of a muscle in which shortening is prevented; muscle length remains the same.

Isotonic muscle contraction is the muscle contraction in which tension developed in less than resistance of load, hence the muscle shortens.

Concentric occurs when the muscle shortens during contraction.

Eccentric occurs when the muscle lengthen during the contraction.

Note: There are two types of isotonic contraction: eccentric and concentric.

275. What are the three effects of hydrotherapy on the body?

Mechanical, thermal and chemical

276. What are the two categories of proprioceptors and where are each located?

Golgi tendon organs and spindle cells. The Golgi tendon organs are located in the tendon near its connection to the muscle and the spindle cells are located mainly in the belly

277. What is a nerve plexus and where is it located?

A nerve plexus is a gathering of nerves and is located outside of the CNS (Central Nervous System.)

278. When you flex the elbow, what becomes the antagonist?   **The triceps**

279. Define muscle atrophy.   **It is a degenerative process due to muscle disease, or lack of use.**

280. What is nephron?   **The functional unit of the kidney.**

281. What are two responses to pain?   **Physical and psychological**

282. Define mechanoreceptors.

Mechanoreceptors are receptors for vibration and for touch.

283. Define organelle.

An organelle is a discrete structure within a cell, having specialized functions, a distinctive chemical composition and identifying molecular structures.

284. What are mitochondria and what do they produce?

Mitochondria are the principal energy source of the cell, and contain

the cytochrome enzymes for releasing energy and converting it to useful forms for cell operation. They produce adenosine 5'-triphosphate.

285. What muscle initiates walking?   **Iliopsoas**

286. There are many muscle groups. What consists of the erector spinal group?
Longissimus, spinalis, and iliocostalis

287. What muscles are involved in mastication?
Masseter, temporalis, medial pterygoid, lateral pterygoid

288. Name the group of muscles of the shoulder?
Latissimus dorsi, teres minor, teres major, deltoid, supraspinatus, infraspinatus and the subscapularis

289. What is the most superficial hamstring muscle?   **The biceps femoris**

290. What is the difference between a sprain and a strain?
A sprain refers to damaged ligaments, and a strain refers to damaged muscles and tendons.

291. Name the types of movable joints in the body.
Condyloid or ellipsoid, saddle, gliding, ball and socket, hinge, and pivot joints.

292. Name three immovable joints in the body.
Suture, gomphosis, and synchondrosis

293. What is synarthroses?   **It is an immovable cartilaginous joint**

294. What does TMJ stand for?   **It is a colloquial for Temporomandibular Joint Dysfunction**

295. What does TNTC stand for?   **Too numerous to count.**

296. Name the divisions of the brain; the smaller & larger portions of the brain.
Celebrum, cerebellum, and the brain stem. The largest portion is the cerebrum and the smaller portion is the cerebellum.

297. What is inflammation and what are the four principal symptoms and signs of inflammation?

Inflammation is a protective and healing response that happens when tissue has been damaged. The 4 principal symptoms are heat, pain, redness and swelling.

298. What are the three layers of connective tissue?

299. What is a subluxation? **An incomplete or partial dislocation**

300. There are several terms used describing body movement. Define the following:

abduction = movement of a limb or body part further from or away from the midline of the body

adduction = movement of a limb or body part closer to or toward the midline of the body

extension = straightening of a joint or extremity so that the angle between contiguous (adjoining) bones is increased

flexion = bending of a joint or extremity so that the angle between contiguous bones is decreased

eversion = movement of turning a body part outward away from the midline

inversion = movement of turning a body part inward toward the midline

pronation = movement of turning a body to face downward or turning the hand so that the palm is facing downward

supination = movement of turning the body to face upward or turning the hand so that the palm faces upward

301. Name at least 5 positions of the body (positioning terminology).
Anatomic, supine, prone, lateral and oblique

302. What is acetylcholine?
A chemical neurotransmitter found at the myoneural junction.

303. What are the names of the 3 abnormal curves of the spine?
Scoliosis, lordosis and kyphosis

304. Where is red bone marrow found and where is yellow bone marrow found?
Red marrow is found in the ends of the long bones and in flat bones i.e.

skull and legs; and yellow marrow is found in the medullary cavity of the long bones

305. There are two types of bone tissue, cancellous and dense. Where are both of these found?

Dense tissue is found on the outer portion of the bone just under the periosteum, and cancellous tissue is found on the interior of flat bones and in the ends of long bones.

306. What are the three most common types of arthritis?

Rheumatoid, osteoarthritis and gouty arthritis

307. Where is the mitral valve located?

Between the left atrium and left ventricle

QUESTIONS ON THE CARDIOVASCULAR SYSTEM AND OTHER MISCELLANEOUS QUESTIONS

1. What is carcinoma?

The most common kind of cancer arises in the epithelium (the layers of cells covering the body's surface of lining internal organs and various glands.

2. What is melanoma?

An increasingly prevalent form of cancer which starts in the pigment cells located among the epithelial cells of the skin.

3. Where do sarcomas originate?

In the supporting (or connective) tissues of the body, such as bones, muscles and blood vessels.

4. Where does leukemia begin?

In the blood-forming tissues - the bone marrow, lymph nodes and spleen.

5. Where are lymphomas born? **In the cells of the lymph system.**

6. Would you massage a patient with cancer?

Not before consulting with physicians who have knowledge of the case.

7. Name the four components of blood.

Red/white blood cells, platelets, and blood plasma

8.   How many beats per minute is the (average) heart rate in an adult?
     75 to 80 per minute

9.   How many chambers are in the heart.   **Four**

10. What is another name for "freckles"?   **Melanocytes**

11. The conductivity of heart tissue is measured by what?   **An electrocardiogram (aka ECG, or EKG)**

12. What does the cerebrum preside over?   **Will, reasoning, and memory**

13. List 16 contraindications.
     High blood pressure
     Low blood pressure
     Varicose veins
     Osteoporosis
     Open sores
     Diabetes
     Any break or infection on the skin
     Cancer
     Burns
     Inflammation
     Fever
     Asthma
     Edema (in some cases)
     Alcohol impairment
     Extreme frailty
     Heart disease

LISTED ARE SOME OF THE NAMES YOU SHOULD BECOME FAMILIAR WITH AS EACH ONE IS IMPORTANT IN THE HISTORY OF MASSAGE

Dolores Krieger	Developed "The Therapeutic Touch" and (1976, April) Nursing research for a new age. Nursing Times,
Jack Meagher	A physical therapist, and pioneer in the field of sports massage (pressure points) who also worked with animals on pressure points
Ruth Rice	A nurse, psychologist, and specialist in early child development developed a specific stroking and massage technique for premature babies.
Iona Marsaa Teeguarden	Researcher of acupressure techniques who developed Jin Shin Do

Pauline E. Sasaki	Teacher of advanced Shiatsu, co-author, translator and known world-wide for her work in Shiatsu
Hippocrates	Father of medicine, the Greek Physician
Bonnie Pruden	Myotherapy
Per Henrik Ling	Swedish massage, credited with developing it
Frances Tappan	Massage for physical therapy
Janet Travell	Trigger points, myofacial work
Milton Trager	Rocking motion, Trager Massage
Hwang Ti	Amma Massage
Albert Hoffa	Short massage in anatomical segments
Elizabeth Dicke	Connective Tissue Massage Therapy
James B. Mennell	Head of Massage Department @ St. Thomas Hospital, London 1934. Wrote a book on the basics of massage therapy.
Ambroise Pare	Founder of modern massage.
Sir William Bennett	In 1899 he re-introduced massage to the medical profession and opened a massage department at St. George's Hospital in London.
Murai and Mary Iino Burmeister	Jin shin jyutsu

NOTE: There are many individuals who have contributed to the massage profession. We suggest subscribing to the Massage & Bodywork Magazine. This magazine has the most current modalities, helpful articles and is an excellent magazine not only for professionals but for students who are preparing for their exams.

THESE TERMS RELATE TO PATHOLOGY

- Acute "lower back pain"
- Adhesions
- Atherosclerosis
- Arteriosclerosis
- AIDS - HIV
- Asthma
- Migraines
- Headaches
- Gastroenteritis
- Constipation
- Sinusitis
- Hernia
- PMS - Pre-menstrual syndrome
- Rotator cuff teat

- Myocardial infarction
- Sciatica
- Kyphosis
- Plantar fascitis
- MS - Multiple Sclerosis
- Osgood-Schlatters
- Leukemia
- Cerebral palsy
- Parkinson's disease
- Spinal cord injury - Para, Quad
- Burns
- Polymyositis
- Hypertension
- Rheumatoid arthritis
- Cystic fibrosis
- Systemic lupus erythematosus
- Congestive heart failure
- Patellofemoral stress syndrome
- Hypertrophic scar

CPR Review

1.   These common actions can lead to choking.
   a.   Drinking alcohol before and during eating
   b.   trying to swallow poorly chewed food
   c.   walking, playing, running with objects in mouth

2.   What is the Heimlich maneuver and please describe it in detail?
   It is the abdominal thrust that is used when a person is choking. There is an upward push to the abdomen given to clear the airway of a person with a complete airway obstruction. You ask the person if they are choking and if they can not respond tell them that you are trained in first aid and offer to help. Stand behind the person. The person may be either sitting or standing. Wrap your arms around their waist. Make a fist with one hand. Place the thumb side of your fist against the middle of the person's abdomen, just above the navel and well below the lower tip of the breastbone. Grasp your fist with your other hand. Keeping your elbows out from the person, press your fist into the person's abdomen with a quick upward thrust. Be sure that your fist is directly on the middle of the midline of the person's abdomen when you press. Do not direct the thrusts to the right or to the left.

Think of each thrust as a separate and distinct attempt to dislodge the object. Repeat the thrusts until the obstruction is cleared or until the person becomes unconscious. I highly suggest you take the American Red Cross Community CPR First Aid Course and review their workbook thoroughly!

3. What is a heart attack?

    It is when one or more of the blood vessels that supply blood to a portion of the heart become blocked. When this happens the blood can't get through to feed that part of the heart. When the flow of oxygen-carrying blood is cut off, the cells of this part of the heart begin to die.

4. If the heart stops what is this called?   **A cardiac arrest**

5. The first aid for a heart attack is to do what?

    Recognize the signals of a heart attack, make the person sit or lie down in a comfortable position, and call the EMS system for help.

ORIGINS, INSERTIONS AND ACTIONS OF MUSCLES

1. What is the insertion of the zygomaticus major?   **Zygomatic bone**

2. What is the insertion of the adductor magnus?   **Linea aspera of femur, and adductor tubercle of femur**

3. What is the insertion of the levator scapula?   **Superior angle of scapula**

4. What is the insertion of the tibialis anterior?   **First cuneiform and the first metatarsal**

5. What is the origin of the temporalis?   **Temporal bone**

6. What is the insertion of the trapezius?

    Base of spine of scapula, clavicle, and acromion

7. What is the insertion of the spinalis thoracis?

    Spines of middle and upper thoracic vertebrae

8. What is the insertion of the vastus medialis?

    Common tendon of quadriceps femoris also referred to as tibial tuberosity, and patella

9.   What is the action of the vastus medialis?
Extends leg and draws patella inward

10.   What is the insertion of the adductor brevis?
Upper third of medial lip of linea aspera of femur (pubis)

11.   What is the insertion of the tensor fascia late?
Iliotibial band of fascia lata

12.   What is the insertion of the extensor digitorum brevis?
To 1st phalanx of great toe and the tendons of extensor digitorum longus, of 4 medial toes (not 5th toe)

13.   What is the insertion of the semimembranosus?
Posterior medial condyle of the tibia

14.   What is the insertion of the pectineus?   **Pectineal line of femur**

15.   What is the insertion of the soleus?   **Calcaneus, by way of the Achilles tendon**

16.   What is the insertion of the depressor anguli oris?   **Angle of mouth**

17.   What is the insertion of the buccinator?   **Orbicularis oris**

18.   What is the insertion of the brachialis?   **Ulnar tuberosity, coronoid process**

19.   What is the insertion of the teres minor?
Inferior facet on greater tubercle of humerus

20.   What is the origin of the teres minor?
Axillary border of scapula

21.   What is the action of the teres minor?   **Rotates arm outward, and extension of humerus**

22.   What is the action of the teres major?
Rotates arm inward, draws it down and back

23.   What is the insertion of the teres major?

Medial lip of the bicipital groove of the humerus

24.   What is the origin of the teres major?

Inferior angle of the scapula

25.   What is action of the pectoralis major?

Flexes, adducts and rotates arm

26.   What is the origin of the pectoralis major?

Sternum, clavicle, and cartilages of 1st through 6th ribs

27.   What is the insertion of the pectoralis major?

Bicipital groove of humerus

28.   What is the insertion of the pectoralis minor?

Coracoid process of scapula

29.   What is the insertion of the supraspinatus?

Greater tubercle of the humerus

30.   What is the action of the infraspinatus?

Extension of humerus and lateral rotation

31.   What is the insertion of the coracobrachialis?

Middle of inner border of humerus

32.   What is the origin of the coracobrachialis?

Coracoid process of scapula (flexion of shoulder)

33.   What is the insertion of the brachioradialis?

Styloid process of radius

34.   What is the origin of the brachioradialis?

Brachioradialis originates from the proximal two thirds of the lateral supracondylar ridge of the humerus, and the anterior surface of the lateral intermuscular septum supracondylar ridge of humerus; sometimes called the shaft of the humerus

35. What is the action of the brachioradialis? **Brachioradialis flexes the elbow. Brachioradialis supinates the forearm**

36. What is the action of the serratus anterior?

    Elevates ribs, and protracts and rotates scapula

37. What is the origin of the serratus anterior?

    Upper 8 ribs

38. What is the insertion of the serratus anterior?

    Angles and vertebral border of scapula

39. The triceps brachii is the only posterior upper arm muscle which consists of three heads (long, lateral, and medial). There are 3 origins. Name these origins.

    (1) infraglenoid tubercle of scapula

    (2) humerus below radial groove

    (3) posterior surface of humerus below great tubercle

40. What are the origins of the posterior, middle, and anterior deltoid's and please answer in that order? **Spine of scapula, acromion, lateral clavicle**

41. What is the action of the peroneus tertius?

    Assists in dorsiflexion and eversion of foot

42. What is the insertion of the peroneus tertius?

    Fifth metatarsal bone

43. What is the origin of the peroneus longus?

    Upper fibula

44. What is the insertion of the peroneus brevis?

    Base of 5th metatarsal bone

45. What is the origin of the vastus lateralis?

    Linea aspera to greater trochanter

46. What is the insertion of the vastus intermedius?

    Patella and via patellar ligament to tibial tuberosity

47. What is the insertion of the lumbricales manus?

First phalanx and extensor tendon

48. What is the action of the abductor pollicis longus?

Abducts and assists in extending the thumb

49. What is the action of the gluteus maximus?

Extends and rotates thigh

50. What is the origin of the gluteus maximus?

Superior curved iliac line and crest, and sacrum

51. What is the insertion of the gluteus minimus?   **Greater trochanter**

52. What is the action of the gluteus medius?

Abducts and rotates the thigh

53. What is the origin of the gracilis?

Symphysis pubis and pubic arch

54. What is the action of the psoas major?

Flexes thigh, adducts and rotates it medially

55. What is the insertion of the psoas minor?

Iliac fascia and iliopectineal tuberosity

56. What is the origin of the psoas major?

Last thoracic and all of the lumbar vertebrae

57. What is the origin of the vastus lateralis?

Linea aspera to greater trochanter

58. What is the insertion of the vastus lateralis?

Patella and via patellar ligament to tibial tuberosity

59. What is the action of the vastus lateralis?

Extends the knee

60.   What is the action of the buccinator?
Compresses cheek, and retracts angle of mouth

61.   What is the action of the following muscles: constrictor pharyngis inferior/medius/superior?
Narrows the pharynx, as in swallowing

62.   What is the origin of the masseter?
Zygomatic arch and malar process of superior maxilla

63.   What is the action of the mentalis?   **Elevates and protrudes the lower lip**

64.   What is the insertion of the mentalis?   **Integument of chin**

65.   What is the action of the iliocostalis cervicis?   **Extends cervical spine**

66.   What is the origin of the iliocostalis cervicis?   **Angles of 3rd to 6th ribs**

67.   What is the action of the iliocostalis lumborum?   **Extends lumbar spine**

68.   What is the insertion of the iliocostalis lumborum?   **In angles of 5th to 12th ribs**

69.   What is the action of interspinales?   **Supports and extends vertebral column**

70.   What is the action of the intertransversarii?   **Flexes vertebral column**

71.   What is the action of the rectus capitis posterior major?
Rotates and draws head backward

72.   What is the origin of the rectus capitis posterior minor?
Posterior tubercle of atlas

73.   What is the insertion of the rectus capitis posterior major?
Inferior curved line of the occipital bone

74.   What is the action of the rectus capitis posterior minor?
Rotates and draws the head backward

75.   What is the action of the cricothyroideus? **Tightens the vocal cords**

76. What is the action of the obliquus externus abdominis?

Contracts abdomen and viscera

77. What is the action of the obliquus internus abdominis?

Obliquus internus abdominus flexes the lumbar vertebral column. Obliquus internus abdominus rotates the lumbar vertebral column to the ipsilateral side.

78. What is the action of the quadratus lumborum?

Flexes the trunk laterally and forward, or raises hip

79. What is the insertion of the quadratus lumborum?

Twelfth rib and the upper lumbar vertebrae

80. What is the origin of the coccygeus?

Ischial spine and sacrospinous ligament

81. What is the action of the coccygeus?

Supports coccyx, and closes pelvic outlet

82. What is the insertion of the coccygeus?

Coccyx and lowest portion of sacrum

83. What is the action of the sphincter ani externus?

Closes anus

84. What is the origin of the piriformis?

Margins of anterior sacral foramina and great sacrosciatic notch of ilium

85. What is the action of the rectus femoris?

Extension of knee and assists flexion of femur at hip

86. What is the origin of the rectus femoris?

Iliac spine, upper margin of acetabulum

87. What is the insertion of the rectus femoris?   **Base of patella**

88. What is the action of the tensor fasciae latae?   **Flexes and rotates the thigh**

89. What is the action of the arrectores pilorum?

Elevates hairs of the skin "goosebumps"

90.   What is the origin of arrectores pilorum?

Papillary layer of skin

91.   What is the action of the sternocleidomastoid muscles?

Rotates and depresses the head, bilateral flexion of neck, unilateral flexion of neck to same side, rotation of head to opposite side

92.   What is the action of the platysma?

Wrinkles skin of neck and chest, and depresses jaw and lower lip

93.   What is the origin of the medial pterygoid?   **Pterygoid plate**

94.   What is the action of the hyoglossus?

Depresses side of tongue and retracts tongue

95.   What is the action of the salpingopharyngeus?

Elevates nasopharynx (the soft palate)

96.   What is the insertion of the salpingopharyngeus?

The posterior portion of the pharyngopalatinus

97.   What is the action of the aryepiglotticus?

Closes glottis opening back of tongue

98.   What is the insertion of the rhomboids minor?

Proximal portion of spine of scapula

99.   What is the insertion of the spinalis cervicis?

Axis and occasionally the two vertebrae below

100.   What does innervation of muscles mean?

The stimulation of a part of the muscle through the action of nerves or the nerve supply of the muscle.

QUESTIONS ON HYDROTHERAPY, APPLICATIONS, ETC.

1. Define hydrotherapy. **Hydrotherapy is the application of water in any of its three forms (vapor, ice, water) to the body for therapeutic purposes.**

2. What is the purpose of the Russian bath and what are some of the benefits?

    The purpose is for causing perspiration as it is a full body steam bath and the benefits are improved metabolism, relaxation and cleansing.

3. What is the average time or duration for a cold bath, sitz bath/shower?

    Approximately three to five minutes

4. What is cryotherapy? **Application of ice for therapeutic purposes**

5. What are three things cold applications do that are beneficial to the body?

    Stimulate nerve, increase activity of body cells, and improve circulation

6. Why would you not endure long periods of cold applications?

    Because they can produce depressing effects

7. What is a contrast bath and what are some of the benefits of a contrast bath?

    A contrast bath is alternating the application of hot and cold baths to a certain part of the body, and they help to increase local circulation. The causes an alternating vasoconstriction and vasodilatation of the blood vessels in the area being worked on.

8. Describe was an application of heat would cause and what a local application of heat would cause.

    The application of heat causes an increase in pulse rate, circulation, and white blood cell count. The local application of heat causes relaxation of local musculature and slight analgesia, increased metabolism and leukocyte migration to the area where heat is being applied.

9. What is a slight analgesia? **It is a neurologic state in which painful stimuli are so moderated that, though still perceived, they are no longer painful.**

10. Give two objectives of hydrotherapy baths.

    Stimulation of bodily functions and external cleanliness.

11.   What are three benefits of having a cabinet bath treatment?
      Cleansing procedure, induce perspiration and relaxation.

12.   Name the three classifications of effects of hydrotherapy on the body.
      Chemical, mechanical and thermal

13.   Give some reasons why the application of ice is beneficial.
      Reduces pain, causes vasoconstriction to limit swelling, acts as an analgesic to reduce pain and is generally beneficial on swollen, inflamed and painful areas.

14.   You should NEVER give hot or cold applications when a person has the following:
      ● **diabetes**
      ● **lung disease**
      ● **kidney infection**
      ● **infectious skin condition**
      ● **cardiac impairment**
      ● **extremely high or low blood pressure**

15.   True or False. Hot water applications improve the condition of the skin by promoting perspiration and by increasing the circulation of the blood to the surface of the skin.   **True**

16.   What would the temperature of a warm bath be in F and in C degrees, and what would the temperature of a hot bath be in F and in C degrees?
      Warm bath is 95 to 100° F which= 35 to 37.7° C.
      Hot bath is 100° to 115° F, which = 37.7 to 43.3° C

17.   What are the three main benefits of a whirlpool bath?
      Soothes the nerves, relaxes the muscles, and increases the blood circulation

18.   The skin can safely tolerate _____°F of hot water and approximately _____ °F of steam vapor.   Water at _____°F over a prolonged period of time would raise the body temperature to a very dangerous level.   Fill in the blanks in order.
      115 ; 140 ; 110

19.   Define a Swedish Shampoo.   **It is a body bath that cleans the body using either a brush or bath mitten solution of mild soap and warm water and is then followed by rinsing and drying the body.**

20. Is it okay to leave a client alone for long periods of time while they are in a cabinet bath?

No, you should always be near your client during water treatments.

21. When is a salt rub usually given?   **After a cabinet bath or after a hot bath. It can even be given as a separate treatment.**

22. Hydrotherapy baths are controlled by three things. What are they?

Proper temperatures, pressure and duration of the treatments

23. What acupressure point would you use on the Lung Meridian to affect the stomach?

L10   NOTE: This question was somewhat ambiguous on the National Exam; however, the L10 Lung channel relates to the stomach, especially with children who have nutrition problems.

24. If a person says they have had depression for a long time and they think getting this massage will cure them, you should:

a. **Suggest counseling and do the massage**

b. refuse the massage

c. Agree that it will cure them

25. What hormone stimulates the thyroid?   **Answer: TSH**

26. What do tendons do?   **Answer: Attach skeletal muscle to bones**

27. What part of the body is yang?   **Upper part**

28. What part of the body is yin?   **Lower part**

29. Is testosterone a steroid hormone?   **Yes**

30. What do you do if you are working on a client and he/she complains of pain where you are working?

Answer: release the pressure until they tell you they are comfortable

31. What are the sense organs?   **Touch, taste, smell, sight and sound**

ATTENTION
The remainder of this book may have some questions that DO NOT have the answers. Each month students send in questions they had on their National Exam and our research team may not have time to fill in the answers. Some of the questions that were sent in during 2006 appear in this section.

1.   What chakra is posterior to scapula?

2.   What chakra is all energy held in?

3.   What is the fourth chakra and what is the color? **Heart, green**

4.   If a runner comes in and complains of patella pain, what do you massage?

5.   What is weak if a client has lordosis?

6.   What joint is a bital joint?

7.   What emotion is associated with wood?

8.   What taste is associate with spleen? **Sweet**

9.   What do you exercise with kyphosis?

10.   What vitamin(s) is(are) water soluable? **C, E**

11.   What is the name of too much subcutaneous tissue?

12.   What is good for osteoporosis? **Calcium**

13.   What muscles are involved in frozen shoulder?

14.   Skin temperature is regulated by what system?

15.   What stroke is good for fibrosis adhesions? **Friction**

16.   What is lympatic drainage good for?

17.   Where does the pulmonary artery take blood to?

18.   When you find an unconscious person, what is the first thing you do?**Call 911**

19.   When giving CPR, when do you stop?

20.   What aromatherapy is good for respiratory problems?
        ALL OF THESE APPLY: Niaoui, peppermint, poppy seed

21.   If one shoulder is higher than the other what is this called?

22.   When does HIV start to replicate?

23.   When you laterally rotate the femur, what muscle shortens?

24.   How does a physician refer a patient to you?

25.   What point would you work on for headaches in Oriental modality?

26.   Crystallized mineral chunks that develop in the urinary tract are called what?

27.   What types of problems can a 40 year old woman have who has had radiation
        therapy and is a survivor of breast cancer?

28.   What is the emotion of the liver according to Chinese theory?

30.   If someone is fearful, restless and has a tendency for edema, which meridian
        would you focus on?

31.   After changing treatment plans several times without a change in outcome,
        how would you continue? It is best to refer the patient to another professional
        who could possiby help.

32.   After massaging a client who has been in the supine position, they still have
        retracted shoulders. Which muslces would you suggest stretching?

33.   What do you do with a client that you've been seeing for several sessions who
        has become repulsive to you lately?

34.   Why would you elevate a limb during massage?

35. What skin condition might be red and flake off during massage?

There were several choices. One was psoriasis which the lady chose. Be sure and research various skin conditions and their appearances, etc.

36. Where does the gall bladder meridian begin?

One option in the multiple choice was : outside cover of eye (this is correct)

37. Where does the spleen meridian begin? **One option was large toe. Correct**

38. What needs to happen to get rid of spasms and cramps in the posterior hamstrings?

Precede massage of hamstrings with anterior contraction of the quads.

39. What Yin organ is paired with the stomach meridian? **Spleen**

40. Which meridian starts in the outside corner of the eye, zigzags and exits at the 4th toe?

Gall bladder

41. What would you send a doctor who has referred a patient to you?

A progress report.

42. What does HARA mean? **A centering place**

43. What organ is related to metal? **Lung/Large Intestine**

44. What meridian is most commonly used for headache relief? **L14**

45. Which organ meridian is typically used for insomnia and memory?

46. What do you need to do if you are going into business with someone else?

Don't tell anyone you are partners. Make sure one of you is spending more money than the other. File a K1 Report to the IRS. These were choices

47. In Ayruvedic practices the following is true:

a. you need to consider the body and mind are separate

b. the emotions have nothing to do with disease

Answer: the body and mind can not be separated

48.   Why does a massage therapist drape a client?

It ensures trust in client and respects client's need for modesty.

49.   Why is the appearance of a massage therapist important?

Answer: to develop trust, confidence and cleanliness

50.   In which layer of skin are the lymph and blood vessels?   **Dermis**

51.   What movement helps the functioning of synovial secretion?   **Friction**

52.   What part of the body is affected by thoracic outflow syndrome?   **Arm and neck**

53.   What does pes anserine mean?

Pain and tenderness on the inside of your knee, just about two inches below the joint, are two of the symptoms of pes anserine bursitis of the knee. The pes anserine bursa is a small lubricating sac located between the shinbone (tibia) and three tendons of the hamstrings muscle at the inside of the knee. Because the three tendons splay out on the front of the shinbone and look like the foot of a goose, pes anserine bursitis is also known as "goose foot" bursitis.

54.   What is the function of neurotransmitters?   **Inhibition**

55.   Bones touching bones are referred to as what?

The student was not sure of the answer however some of the multiple choices were: mushy ends, hard ends, soft ends, lux ends and 'grades of moulding'. In the medical profession, grades of moulding is a term used sometimes when bones are touching bones.

56.   What is another name for SOMA?   **Cell body**

57.   What systems insure homeostasis?   Respiratory and circulatory   (The choices listed 2 paired systems together for an answer but the student chose ice the above answer)

58.   What does it mean to have NET income?   **Money minus deductions**

59.   What oil type is least likely to stain sheets?   **Water dispersable**

60.   Therapists avoid injury to themselves by doing what?

Distributing their weight evenly between forward and back foot.

61.   What muscle is affected when toenails curve up into shoe?

    a.   Extensor digitorum

    b.   Extensor digitorum longus (correct)

    c.   Extensor carpi ulnaris

62.   Where does the bladder meridian/channel start?

    a.   Inner canthus of eye (correct)

    b.   Lateral little finger

63.   In Chinese medicine, what organ is affected by edema, impotence, loss of memory?

    a.   Lung

    b.   Heart

    c.   Kidney (correct)

    d.   Spleen

64.   In what case would a doctor advise a "comfort order"?

    a.   Discharge a patient

    b.   For the terminally ill (correct)

    c.   Admit a patient

65.   What joint is affected by inguinal pain?

    a.   Hip (correct)

    b.   Knee

    c.   Wrist

    d.   Shoulder

66.   If giving massage as barter, how much income do you report?

Be sure and ask your instructors about this question. A student who sent in this question did not know the answer. The choices:

    a.   0%

    b.   5%

    c.   80%

    d.   100% (correct)

67.   How would you position arm to massage serratus anterior?

    a.   Horizontally adduct

    b.   Horizontally abduct (correct)

    c.   Medially rotate humerus

68.   How do you position pregnant woman in 3rd trimester?

    a.   Prone

    b.   Supine (correct)

    c.   Side-lying

69.   What condition results in degenerative muscle turning into fatty tissue?

    a.   Muscular dystrophy (correct)

    b.   Multiple sclerosis

    c.   Fibrosis

    d .   Other

70.   What is the term for one cycle of normal inspiration and normal expiration?

    a.   Vial capacity

    b.   Residual volume

    c.   Tidal volume (correct)

    d.   Total capacity

71.   What is an aponeurosis?

Fibrous or membranous sheet connecting a muscle and the part it moves.

72.   Where does the kidney meridian/channel start?

Under the 5th toe and runs to the sole of the foot

73.   Where does the pericardium channel/meridian start?

It originates from the chest and enters the pericardium, then descends through the diaphragm to the abdomen to communicate with the upper, middle and lower Burner.

74.   Where does the gall-bladder channel/meridian start?

At the outer canthus of the eye

75.   Where does the liver channel/meridian start?

On the big toe and runs upwards on the dorsum of the foot and medial malleolus, and then up the medial aspect of the leg.

76.   From where does the Direction Vessel originate?

The uterus (or deep in the lower abdomen in men) and emerges at the perineum.

77. The yang organs transform, digest & excrete impure products of what?
Food and Fluids

78. The yin organs store the pure essences resulting from the process of transformation carried out by what?   **The Yang organs**

79. The 5 yin organs store vital substances i.e. what?
Qi, blood, body fluids and essence

80. Do the 6 yang organs transform, digest, or store?
They transform and digest.

81. Yang transforms what?   **Qi**

82. Yin forms the _____.   **Structure**

83. The liver has a couple of functions. What are they?
Stores blood and keeps the blood moving, ensuring the smooth flow of Qi all over the body

84. Are yin and yang in a constant state of change?   Yes or no?   **Yes**

85. In Chinese Medicine, balance in life is the essence of prevention. Know what some of the things that constitute this balance? Some are:
Sexual life,   Exercise,   Diet,   Work

86. What constitutes the basis of Chinese Medical theory?   **The 5 elements**

87. What is the brachial plexus?
It is a network of nerves. It conducts signals from the spine to the arm and hand. These signals cause the arm and hand muscles to move.

88. What is the normal craniosacral rate?
The craniosacral rate refers to the rhythmic movement of cerebrospinal fluid. It is a wavelike motion with a rhythm that ranges from 6 to 10 cycles per minute. Cranial therapists are trained to detect abnormalities in this rhythm by palpating suture lines of the skull, detecting abnormalities in pressure, rhythm and flow.

89. What muscle lies over the sciatic notch?   **Piriformis**

90. Why is the hypoglossal canal sometimes named the anterior condylar canal?
Because it lies just anterior to the occipital condyle

91. What are some of the muscles that are weakened in a client who has Lordosis?
Abdominal

92. What acupressure point would you use on the Lung meridian to reduce a headache? **L14**

93. What does a practitioner need in order to send a client's health records to another health professional? **A signed medical release form**

94. Certain lotions can irritate what system? **Integumentary (Skin)**

95. What would happen if you applied pressure on the carotid?
It can slow the heart rate or cut off blood supply to the head, causing dizziness of black outs.

96. Bilateral Contraction of the Iliopsoas would cause what affect? **Stooping posture**

97. How would you support an injured joint while doing a massage treatment?
With pillows and bolster

98. Where would you place a pillow if your client were in a prone position with complaint of lower back pain? **One student sent in the answer Abdomen (This question was sent in by several students so be sure and know the correct answer)**

99. During the initial assessment, what activity should be performed in order to gather information on a clients' joint mobility? **Active ROM**

100. Increase in the lumen of a vessel is called what? **Vasodilatation**

101. What muscle contributes to your client wearing a hole in the top of their shoe by their big toe? **Extensor Hallucis Longus**

102. Note: THERE WERE SEVERAL QUESTIONS ON FRICTION STROKE.
(Reduces myofascial restrictions)

103. What massage stroke stretches and broadens muscles? **Cross Fiber Friction**

104. DON'T EVER DIAGNOSE A CLIENT'S CONDITION BEFORE, DURING OR AFTER A MASSAGE; HOWEVER, YOU CAN SUGGEST THEY SEE A D.O. OR SOMEONE WHO IS KNOWLEDGEABLE ABOUT A CONDITION THAT YOU ARE NOT KNOWLEDGEABLE ABOUT.

105. How does energy flow? Up and down, In or out, side to side, or front to back?
Up and down is the correct answer.

106. How would you treat an abrasion of the leg? Several choices were: heat, cold, cream.
Answer: AVOID THE AREA, DON'T TREAT

107. How do cold compresses reduce pain? **Decreases sensory impulses**

108. During a massage session the practitioner palpates a small lump under a clients chin. What can the therapist surmise it might be?
a. swollen lymph node
b. scar tissue (Scar tissue is the correct answer)
c. tumor

109. What organ controls emotions?

110. How does Governing Energy Flow? **Base of spine to upper lip.**

111. Know where meridian energy begins and ends.

112. What system(s) control homeostasis in the body?
8 vessels

113. When doing a facial massage what should the therapist be mindful of?
Never apply too much pressure on the facial muscles, and no pressure over the eyes.

114. What vitamins would help the retina of the eye?
A, and possibly D and E

115. What type of exercise would help with Osteoporosis? **Weight bearing exercises**

116. What helps build hemoglobin in the red blood cells? **Iron**

117. What stance would a therapist move into when working on the quadratus lumborum?

45 degree angle of approach.

118. When doing lymphatic drainage, what direction would a therapist massage to facilitate lymph drainage? **Toward the lymph nodes, center of body or medially**

119. What can lymphatic drainage cause? **Increase in vascular circulation**

120. How does a therapist determine the minutes of a treatment?

Choices were: depends on how much money the client has, the therapist tells the client how long the appointments last, etc.

121. What is the term used when the arm moves towards the body? **Adduction**

122. In *whiplash*, what muscles are affected? **Posterior neck muscles**

123. What are some psychological effects of massage?

Massage generally increases feelings of relaxation and well-being in patients. Whether this is from placebo effect or the result of some previously undiscovered reflex is not fully understood. Practitioners often incorporate a variety of psychophysical techniques, such as guided imagery, into massage treatment.

124. What are the eight vessels in oriental medicine and explain a little about their history.

The eight vessels are called "Qi Jing Ba Mai." Qi means odd, strange, or mysterious. Jing means meridian or channels. Ba means eight and Mai means vessels. Qi Jing Ba Mai is then trans lated as "Odd Meridians and Eight Vessels" or "Extraordinary Meridians (EM)." "Odd" has a meaning of strange in Chinese. It is used simply because these eight vessels are not well understood yet. Many Chinese doctors explain that they are called "Odd" simply because there are four vessels that are not paired. Since these eight vessels also contribute to the maintenance of homeostasis, some times they are called "Homeostatic Meridians." These vessels are: Governing Vessel; Conception Vessel (Du Mai) and Conception Vessel (Ren Mai); Thrusting Vessel; Girdle Vessel; Yang Heel Vessel; Yin Heel Vessel; Yang Linking Vessel; and Yin Linking Vessel.

125. What does the Governing Vessel control?

The Governing Vessel controls all the Yang channels. It flows up the midline of the back, a Yang area, and in the center of all Yang channels (except the stomach channel which flows in the front). The Governing Vessel governs all the Yang channels, which means that it can be used to increase the Yang energy of the body. Since the Governing

Vessel controls or governs the back, the area richest in Qi, it is also responsible for the circulation of the body's energy.

126.   What is the function of the Conception Vessel?

The "Conception Vessel," has a major role in Qi circulation, monitoring and directing all of the Yin channels (plus the stomach channel). The Conception Vessel is connected to the Thrusting and Yin Linking vessels, and is able to increase the Yin energy of the body.

127.   What is one of the major purposes of the Thrusting Vessel?

One of the major purposes of the Thrusting vessel is to connect, to communicate, and to mutually support the Conception vessel. Because of this mutual Qi support, both can effectively regulate the Qi in the kidney channel. The kidneys are the residence of Original Qi and are considered one of the most vital Yin organs.

128.   What is the major purpose of the Girdle Vessel?

The major purpose of the Girdle vessel is to regulate the Qi of the gall bladder. It is also responsible for the Qi's horizontal balance. If you have lost this balance, you will have lost your center and balance both mentally and physically. The Girdle vessel is also responsible for the strength of the waist area. When Qi is full and circulating smoothly, back pain will be avoided.

129.   NOTE: While the preceding four vessels (Governing, Conception, Thrusting, and Girdle) are located in the trunk, the Yang Heel Vessel and the next three are located in the trunk and legs. (In addition, each of these four vessels is paired.) You can see from the way that the Yang Heel vessel intersects with other Qi channels that it regulates the Yang channels, such as the urinary bladder, the gall bladder, the small intestine, and the large intestine.

The Yang Heel vessel is also connected with the Governing vessel. The Qi filling this vessel is supplied mainly through exercising the legs, which converts the food essence or fat stored in the legs. This Qi is then led upward to nourish the Yang channels. It is believed in Qigong that, since this vessel is also connected with your brain, certain leg exercises can be used to cure headaches. Since a headache is caused by excess Qi in the head, exercising the legs will draw this Qi downward to the leg muscles and relieve the pressure in the head.

130.   Define meridian and name the meridians.

Meridian is a general term of the channels and their collaterals. Jing (channels) in Chinese means "route". They are the longitudinal main lines. Luo (collaterals) in Chinese means the network, the branches of the channels reaching every part of the body. Meridians act as the important route for circulating Qi and blood, connecting viscera with extremities, communication of the upper with the lower and the interior with the exterior. Channels take a definite course in the body while collaterals crisscross and are distributed all over the

body, connecting and joining the tissues, organs, orifices, skin, flesh, tendons, and bones of the whole body which build up an organic entity.

1. Governing Vessel   2. Large Intestine   3. Conception Vessel   4. Kidney

6. Heart   7. Stomach   8. Kidney   9. Spleen   10. Liver   11. Lung

12. Gall Bladder   14. Governing Vessel   15. Bladder (inner line)

16. Bladder (outer line)   17. Small Intestine   18. San Jiao

131. There are many ways in which Yin and Yang can be out of balance. List some types of Imbalance between Yin and Yang *Too much Yin*--characterized by Cold symptoms *Too much Yang*--characterized by Heat symptoms *Too little Yin*--characterized by Internal Heat symptoms *Too little Yang*--characterized by general coldness

132. If a client has plantar fasciitis how would you treat this condition?

Postural rebalancing is necessary to take the stress off the area. Lengthening the calf muscles, hip flexors, hip rotators, TFL's, psoas, usually helps. With client supine, the therapist standing at foot of treatment table facing bottom of foot, therapist would grasp client's toes and ball of foot with one hand and dorsiflex foot, stretching plantar fascia; and with the other hand would use their knuckle to strip plantar fascia from the top to the bottom covering all surface areas. Move in the following direction: top ball of foot to the bottom heel. Repeat until condition improved. Be sure to apply as much pressure as your client can take.

133. What is the difference between a sprain and a strain?

A Strain is the tearing of a muscle and/or tendon.

A Sprain is the tearing of a ligament.

134. What is difference between tendonitis and tenosynovitis?

Tendonitis is the inflammation of a tendon. Tenosynovitis is the inflammation of the gliding surface of the tendon and the surrounding sheath. Sheathed tendons are usually found in the wrist and ankles where tendons pass close to the bone.

135. What is the definition of Calcific tendonitis?

Calcific tendonitis is calcium deposits in the tendon usually due to chronic inflammation.

136. True or False. Reflexive physiological effects are generally a result of nervous system responses. **True**

137. What is the best massage stroke to be used on a chronic sprain? **Transverse friction**

138. What are antagonist muscles?

It is the group of muscles opposing a group of contracting muscles.

139. Name the muscles of the back.
   - **Deltoid**
   - **Erector spinae - Spinalis**
   - **Erector spinae - Iliocostalis**
   - **Erector spinae - Longissimus**
   - **Infraspinatus**
   - **Interspinales**
   - **Intertransversarii**
   - **Latissimus dorsi**
   - **Levator scapulae**
   - **Levatores costarum**
   - **Obliquus capitis inferior**
   - **Obliquus capitis superior**
   - **Rectus capitus posterior major**
   - **Rectus capitus posterior minor**
   - **Rhomboid major**
   - **Rhomboid minor**
   - **Serratus posterior inferior**
   - **Serratus posterior superior**
   - **Splenius capitis**
   - **Splenius cervicis**
   - **Supraspinatus**
   - **Teres major**
   - **Teres minor**
   - **Transversospinalis - Multifidus**
   - **Transversospinalis - Rotatores**
   - **Transversospinalis - Semispinalis**
   - **Trapezius**
   - **Quadratus Lumborum**

140. What is ischemia? **It is lack of blood in an area.**

141. What are the borders of the femoral triangle?

Inguinal ligament, sartorius and adductor longus

142. When the muscle spindle cell is over extended too far, what tendon does it engage? **The Golgi tendon organ**

143.   What does the reciprocal inhibition refer to?

It refers to the fact that when one group of muscles contract, the opposite group of muscles relax.

144.   What are the three stages of inflammation?

Acute, subacute and chronic

145.   What is the meaning of Reflexive Physiological Effects?

They are generally a result of the nervous system responses.

146.   Define proprioception.

It is the body's ability to receive information from tendons, muscles, and other frameworks regarding their external and internal conditions.

147.   What is the gate theory?

It is a theory used to describe how pain signals travel slower to the brain than pressure, touch, vibration, and temperature signals

148.   What is the definition of hypoxia?

It is lack of oxygen.

149.   What is one of the purposes of performing the petrissage stoke?

It helps in the venous return.

150.   List the muscles of the abdomen.
- **Diaphragm**
- **External oblique abdominis**
- **Internal oblique abdominis**
- **Psoas major**
- **Psoas minor**
- **Pyramidalis**
- **Quadratus lumborum**
- **Rectus abdominis**
- **Transversus abdominis**

151.   What are some unfavorable conditions associated with hydrotherapy?

Heart palpations, insomnia, hyperventilation, vertigo, shivering, fainting, nausea and headaches

152. Describe the Chinese Organs and their major functions.

KIDNEY - Yin Organ **Stores Jing/Essence Governs birth, growth, development, reproduction, maturation, aging Produces marrow, governs bones, fills the brain with marrow Receives (grasps) Qi Governs fluid production and function Houses the Zhi or Will Source of all Yin and Yang in the body**

LIVER - Yin Organ **Ensures smooth flow of Qi in the entire body Stores and regulates Blood Nourishes and controls sinews (ligaments, tendons, nerves) Houses the Hun or Eternal soul The General in Charge of Planning**

HEART - Yin Organ **The Supreme Commander Governs the blood and blood vesels** *Houses the Shen or mind (waking consciousness)*

SPLEEN - Yin Organ **Governs transformation and transportation Contains blood in the blood vessels Controls and nourishes muscles and limbs Ascends Qi Regulates damp**

LUNG - Yin Organ **The Master of Qi Governs respiration Descends and disperses Qi inthe body Regulates water passages Governs the skin and the body hair Houses the Po or corporeal soul**

153. List the YANG ORGANS and what they are predominantly involved in.

Bladder, Gallbladder, Stomach, Large and Small Intestines. These are the hollow organs. They are predominantly involved in processing of nutrients and excretion of wastes.

154. The Five Elements in Oriental Medicine are:

Water, Wood, Fire, Earth, and Metal.

155. Does this female fit the yin or yang?[1] A 35 year old female complains of having 1) no energy. When not working she sleeps most of the time. 2) She feels cold often and is uncomfortably sensitive to cool environments. 3) Her skin appears damp. 4) She feels dull emotionally and intellectually. 5) Her posture is poor with shoulders that slope forward giving the appearance of a caved-in chest. 6) When she speaks only her lips move. 7) She has been having less contact with her friends, preferring to be alone. DOES SHE FIT YIN OR YANG?

Here is a classification of her symptoms by Yin & Yang characteristics. You can check them against the list of characteristics you just read. 1) stillness 2) cool/cold 3) moist 4) passive 5) inward 6) stillness 7) inward Diagnosis: excess Yin or deficient Yang - depending on the severity of signs. Treatment: Disperse excess Yin or Tonify deficient Yang

156. In Traditional Chinese Medicine there are at least seven very commonly used groups of acu-points. Name these points.

- **Transporting Points**
- **Five Element Points**
- **Xi-Xleft- Accumulating Points**

- **Yuan - Source Qi Points**
- **Mu - Front - Alarm Points**
- **Shu - Back Points**
- **Windows to the Sky or Heaven**

157. Name one artery that contributes to the blood supply of the uterus [besides the uterine artery from the internal iliac], and tell where it originates.

It is the ovarian artery from the aorta at L2.

158. As the external oblique arises it interdigitates with two other muscles. Which two are these and on what ribs? **The last four ribs [latissimus dorsi] and ribs 5,6,7,8 [serratus anterior].**

159. What are nodes of Ranvier? **Gaps between mylein sheath cells**

160. True or False. Mylein could be described as being similar to the insulation of an electrical wire.

True

161. What is the definition of synapse?

It is a small gap between the presynaptic and postsynaptic membranes.

162. What is the difference between the cerebellum and the cerebrum?

The cerebellum is similar to the body's autopilot and the cerebrum is the largest part of the brain.

163. What does the somatic nervous system do?

Allows the control of skeletal muscles.

164. What is myelitis? **It is inflammation of the spinal cord or bone marrow.**

165. What is myeloblast? **It is an embryonic (immature) bone marrow cell.**

166. What is calciuria? **It is the presence of calcium in the urine.**

167. Define the following: complete fracture, compound fracture, greenstick fracture and comminuted fracture.

A complete fracture is with the break across the entire width of a bone; a compound fracture is when the bone protrudes through the skin; a greenstick fracture is when the bone is fractured on one side only; and a comminuted fracture is when the bone is fractured into many pieces.

168. What are osteoblasts?   **Cells that arise from fibroblasts and when they mature they are associated with production of bone.**

169. What are phalanges? What are tarsals?

    Phalanges are fingers or toes. Tarsals are ankle bones.

170. What is lactic acid?   **It is the product of anaerobic cell respiration.**

171. What are synergistic muscles?

    They are muscles that have the same function, acting together.

172. What are antagonistic muscles?

    They are muscles that have the opposite functions.

173. Hormones are made up from three groups. What are these groups?

    Amines, Proteins and Steroids.

174. How many vertebrae are there in each region? Name the movements at each level, and tell what determines the movements.

    Cervical: 7, Flexion, extension, lateral flexion, rotation only at atlanto-axial

    Thoracis: 12, rotation; Lumbar: 5, flexion, extension, lateral flexion

    Sacral: 5 [fused] no movements

    Coccygeal: 4

175. What muscle holds down the 12th rib on respiration?   **The Quadratus lumborum**

176. Is the knee proximal to the foot?   **Yes**

177. Do the cells of the liver detoxify poisons?   **Yes**

178. What is the outer most portion of a cell called?   **Plasma membrane**

179. What is the part of the neuron that receives impulses?   **Dendrite**

180. Where do you find rugae?   **Stomach**

181. Is areolar an epithelial tissue?   **No**

182. The correct order that food passes through the small intestine is what?
Duodenum, jejunum, ileum

183. Where are the islets of Langerhans found?   **Pancreas**

184. True or False. The main exocrine function of the pancreas is to regulate blood sugar levels?
False

185. Which cranial nerve innervates abdominal and thoracic viscera?
No. 10 Vagus nerve

186. Where is oxytocin produced?   **In the hypothalamus**

187. If a client has a muscle spasm, what would one cause be?   **Calcium deficiency**

188. In western anatomical position, the atlas lays inferior to what?
Occipital condyle

189. If someone has a herniated disc, which motion would be contraindicated?
Some of the choices were: rotation, extension, flexion, lateral rotation, AND other

190. If a client is supine and the femur is abducted, what muscle will shorten?
Tensor fascia lata

191. Where does the conception vessel flow up from?

192. If the medial side of the foot drops, what is this know as? **Eversiln**

193. When should you wash the linens used by clients?   **After each use**

194. What is it called when a client has an emotional release during a massage?

195. What covers the digestive system?

196. You have just finished giving a massage and the client is supine. Upon notice the shoulders are lifted off the table. What might you ask the client to do? **Doorway stretch**

197. Why does a cut in the scalp bleed so profusely?

Because the vessels are held open by the connective tissue under the skin and they bleed from both cut ends.

198. What is so unusual about the alveolar bone?

It absorbs pressure on the teeth during mastication without causing re-   absorption of bone. The term alveolar bone can best be described as a thin layer of compact bone that forms the tooth socket surrounding the roots of teeth.

199. Is the common extensor origin on the anterior or posterior surface of the lateral epicondyle of the humerus?   **It is on the anterior surface**

200. What two joints do the hamstrings act upon?

201. True or False. The biceps femoris can also rotate the extended knee.   **False, can only rotate flexed knee**

202. True or False. The biceps femoris Flexes and laterally rotates knee.   **True**

203. Fill in the blanks. The costoclavicular ligament attaches the _____
Clavicle to the first rib

204. How does the gluteus maximus help to hold the knee extended?
By inserting into the iliotibial tract

205. What part of which adductor muscle is supplied by the tibial portion of the sciatic nerve?
The hamstring portion of the adductor magnus

206. What are the six different types of movement at the shoulder joint?
Flexion - Extension - Abduction - Adduction - Rotation - circumduction

207. Does inversion/eversion occur at the ankle joint?
No. It occurs about the axis of rotation of the subtalar joint

208. Name the Yin organs. **Heart, Liver, Lungs, Spleen, Kidneys, Pericardium**

209. What type of massage stroke should be used in acute (non-infection) stage after injury?

   a. light gliding   **b. wait until subacute stage**   c. other

210. What type of oil should be used during massage?

   a. non-scented oil   b. rose water oil   c. other

211. Is the following referred to as energy balancing?

   Yes, Placing one hand on the client's head and the other on the sacrum

212. Know the layers of the skin.

   i.e. Epidermis - Dermis - Subcutaneous.

213. Should the massage therapist ask the client what type of music they prefer?

   Yes, it would be considerate as they may prefer no music

214. If a massage therapist purchases a massage table before obtaining a license, what % will be for tax when he/she starts practicing legally?

   a. nothing   b. 10%   **c. 100%**   d. other

215. In holistic/complementary medicine, homeopathy refers to the Law of similar. True or False

   True

216. If you are performing ROM on a client and you hear a 'click' on top of the shoulder, where would the 'click' be coming from? **Rotator Cuff**

217. True/False.   Shoulder joint is the only one ball>socket type joint. **False**

218. True/False.   Rotator cuff help stabilize humerus. **True**

219. Does impingement occur when rotator cuff muscles are weak? **Yes**

220. Is the back hand exercise an internal rotation type of exercise? **No**

221. Should you always carry heavy objects close to you?   **Yes**

222. Where is the mediastinum?   **In the thoracic cavity**

223. True or False. If you have a client with hypothyroidism they may require a room with a slightly warmer temperature.   **True**

224. What part of the nervous system would relate to the 'fight-or-flight' response to stress?

   The sympathetic

225.   Does a moist heat compress produce muscle relaxation?   **Yes**

226.   If a lateral sprain occurs with the ankle what is the position of the ankle for this sprain to occur?

Inverted

227.   Would you do heavy percussion over the kidney area?   **No**

228.   True or false.   The psoas muscle is located in the cranial cavity.

False. It is located in the abdominal cavity.

229.   What is one of the functions of the nasal cavity?

Warms and moisturizes inspired air and removing debris.

230.   When working in the inguinal ligament region, what must you be aware of being a potential endangerment to?   **Femoral Nerve**

231.   Where do you palpatate the medial longitudinal arch?   **1ˢᵗ metatarsal to calcaneus**

232.   True or False. Massage can help lower blood levels of the parathyroid hormone which is a stress related substance.   **False. It is epinephrine.**

233.   Is the elbow proximal to the wrist?   **Yes**

234.   Does the stomach channel begin below and in line with the pupil?   **Yes**

235.   What is the medial epicondyle of the humerus?

It is the bondy prominence palpable on the medial side of the elbow.

236.   Define what antagonist is.

It describes a muscle who contraction produces a joint action opposite to the joint action of another muscle.

237.   What massage do you do when someone is sensitive to touch?   **Reiki**

238.   The root chakra is associated with what sense?   **Smell**

239.   What hormone does the pineal gland produce?   **Melatonin**

240.   What is similar to marmas?   **Acupuncture points**

241.   What is Chi Nei Tsang?

A Chinese system of deep healing of the use of energy to the five major systems in the body which are: vascular, lymphatic, nervous, and acupuncture meridians.

242.   What is the most common cartilage in the body?   **Hyaline**

243.   Massage of _____ muscle group would be effective in relieving sciatica?
       Gluteus group

QUESTIONS SENT IN NOVEMBER 2007

1.   True or False. Is it possible to drink too much water? **True**

2.   What is hyponatremia? **A condition caused by the dilution of sodium within the body from drinking too much water.**

3.   _____ is a systematic process of gathering information. **Assessment**

4.   What does a pre-event massage do for athletes? **The massage warms the body so it can help prevent injuries.**

5.   Why is a post event massage recommended? **Helps to cool down the athlete's body and rid the body of possible toxins and lactic acid.**

6.   List the 5 steps to the Needs Assessment when dealing with customer service with every client.

      Find the need, to ensure the client feels understood, repeat back what was said; expand possibilities through up-servicing and promotional offerings; the what-why-how method of service recommendations; tell clients when you need to see them again.

7.   What makes Ayurveda unique? **It is the science based upon individuality of the client; one treatment is not right for everyone.**

8.   What are trauma triggers? **They can be anything that causes energy to go through a restricted tissue area and essentially wake it up.**

9.   When does REM sleep first occur? **Usually about 90 minutes after you fall asleep.**

10.   True or False.   When there is kinesthetic dysfunction, you can not accurately sense whether certain muscles are relaxed or tense. **True**

11.   What are the most common types of sleep disorders? **Insomnia, narcolepsy, restless-leg-syndrome, parasomnias, obstructive sleep apnea, central sleep apnea.**

12.   True or False.   A dysfunctional muscle will contract, but it will not return to its normal shape following contraction. **True**

13.   What are the three exercises recommended in order to maintain correct posture?   **The doorway stretch, the deltoid stretch, and the triceps and latissumus dorsi stretch**

14.   What stage of sleep does dreaming occur?   **REM**

15.   _____ _____ is how we sense our body.   **Kinesthetic awareness**

16.   What receptors in your muscles, tendons, and joints inform the brain about the position, shape, effort and direction of your body's movement?   **Proprioceptors**

17.   True or False.   It is relatively easy to observe and discern whether your client's breathing is functional or dysfunctional.   **True**

18.   How well or how poorly your breathing is, is not just a matter of how well oxygen is being supplied to your lungs, but breathing also directly influences what else?

    Your mood, digestion, the efficiency of the functioning of your brain and nervous system, the balance of calcium and magnesium in your body, pain sensitivity, the tone of our muscles, how many active trigger points you have, and how tired or alert you feel.

19.   True or false. It is important for massage therapists to understand how pharmaceutical medications might interact with massage therapy.   **True**

20.   The three main classes of synthetic drugs used as sedatives and hypnotics are: ____ ____ ____.

    Benzodiazepine, Barbiturates, and Non benzodiazepine and non barbiturates.

21.   List of side effects of the benzodiazepines are:

    Fatigue, muscle weakness, dry mouth, nausea and vomiting, dizziness, hangover effect, daytime sedation, rebound insomnia

    The Adverse Effects are:

    Amnesia, Ataxia, Drug abuse, Drug tolerance, Drug dependence

22.   List of side effects of barbiturates are:

    Drowsiness, lethargy, hypotension, vertigo, headache, nausea and vomiting, diarrhea, epigastric pain

    Adverse effects are:

    Depression, Drug dependence, Drug abuse, Drug tolerance,

Hypoventilation, Spasm of the larynx and bronchi, Respiratory depression, Allergic reaction

23.   List of side effects of nonbenzodiazepin – nonbarbiturates

Dizziness, drowsiness, lethargy, hangover effects, gastric irritation, nausea and vomiting, hypotension

Adverse effects are:

Respiratory arrest, Respiratory depression

1.   The tubes that carry urine from the kidney to the bladder are _____.
     Ureters

2.   What are neurotransmitters?   **Chemical messengers**

3.   What hormone does the pineal gland produce?   **Melatonin**

4.   The 1099 Tax Form is used to notify the IRS of _____information?
     Independent Contractor Wages

5.   What is similar to marmas?   **Acupuncture points**

6.   What is more important in taking a Continuing Education Program?
     a.   Learning something new to enhance professional development
     b.   To become certified in order to gain more clients, respect and more money
     c.   I like the instructor

7.   What is Zero Balancing?
     Zero Balancing is a modality that helps relieve physical and mental symptoms; to improve the ability to deal with life stresses; to organize vibratory fields thereby promoting the sense of wholeness and well being.

8.   What is Somatic Resonance?
     It is where the therapist is grounded in their bodily awareness and experience.

9.   What is one of the most challenging skills in massage?
     a.   listening to our hands while we work and the ability to palpate and respond to the individual tissue variances
     b.   scheduling appointments c. doing your taxes

10. What is Chi Nei Tsang?
     A Chinese system of deep healing of the use of energy to the five major systems in the body which are: vascular, lymphatic, nervous, and acupuncture meridians.

11. Hereditary information is stored in the _____.   **Nucleus**

12. Which connective tissue is strong in all directions?
     Dense, irregular, collagenous connective tissue

13.   What is the most common cartilage in the body?   **Hyaline**

14.   Which layer of the skin acts as an energy storehouse?   **Hypodermis**

15.   If your finger is bleeding, you know that the cut is at least as deep as the
_____.   **Dermis**

16.   What is the most lethal form of skin cancer?   **Melanoma**

17.   Where are adipose cells found?   **In the hypodermis**

18.   Which joint is found between the radius and ulna in the antebrachium?
Radioulnar joint

19.   What is the most common type of joint found in the body?   **Synovial**

20.   Fill in the blank by completing the following sequence: abdominal aorta,
common iliac artery, _____, femoral artery.   **External iliac artery**

21.   A deficiency of dietary iodine results in the development of _____.   **A
goiter**

22.   Which movement should be avoided for someone with a hip replacement?
Abduction of the hip

23.   Massage of _____ muscle group would be effective in relieving sciatica?
Gluteus group

24.   What causes poliomyelitis?   **A viral infection**

25.   The mitral valve is also known as the _____?   **Bicuspid valve**

26.   What are warts?
A contagious infection of the epidermis layer of the skin

27.   Proper draping is a very important part of professional business ethics. Why is
this so?
It ensures your client's privacy and comfort

28.   Which muscle attaches to the zygomatic arch?   **Masseter**

29. Can massage reduce pain and if so, in what way?

    Yes. It reduces the cause behind pain stimulation.

30. When you roll a bowling ball forward, what is the primary movement of the shoulder?

    Flexion

31. When you stand on your tip-toes your ankle joint goes through_____.

    Plantarflexion

32. What action are the erector spinae muscles capable of? **Extension**

33. What muscle of the transversospinalis group is found primarily on the cervical and upper thoracic spine? **Semispinalis**

34. What type of joint is located between two adjacent vertebrae? **Symphysis**

35. _____ is the layer of dense irregular connective tissue that is around all bones.

    Periosteum

36. True or False. Type I Diabetes Mellitus is characterized by a deficiency of insulin production by the beta cells within the pancreatic islet cells. **True**

37. True or False. CST (CranioSacral Therapy) works through the crainosacral system to facilitate the performance of the body's inherent self-corrective mechanisms and thereby normalizes the environment in which the central nervous system functions. **True**

38. How many milligrams of magnesium per day should a massage therapist or anyone else for that matter consume? **400 to 800 milligrams to supplement your diet**

39. What are the three steps in helping your clients with chronic pain?

    Understand the emotional dimension of chronic pain; help your client realize other healing resources i.e. acupuncture, yoga, etc.; and create a safe space so your client feels safe, learn body language, move slowly, respect the boundaries of the client and don't impose your own ideas of what the session should be like.

40. True or False. On your intake form referencing pain with 0 being no pain and 10 being worse pain, would you, as a therapist, ask about emotional (psychological) Pain? **True**

41.   Name the five types of scars.
       Hypertrophic, keloid, trama, surgical, and burn

42.   What system is the key to restoring muscle memory? **Circulatory system**

43.   What are the two most common joint problems that massage therapists treat?
       Osteoarthritis and rheumatoid arthritis.

44.   What are seven steps in setting up a safe and effective work area?
       Create comfort by providing all the necessary toiletries i.e. clean sheets, drinking water, make sure the room temperature is comfortable, have controlled lighting, ensure privacy, have a neat treatment room, have a clock in your room that is silent, make sure all equipment is set up properly and in working condition, make the room secure for yourself, as well as for your client.

More Questions from 2007 Exams

45.   Know the Chinese body clock; which organs go with which taste/smell.

46.   1099 Forms; What is the dollar amount that you have to be paid by someone before they are required to issue a 1099 to you? **$600.00**

47.   Know the names of the layers of the skin. **Epidermis, dermis, and subcutaneous fat later**

48.   Know the difference between burns of the 1st, 2nd and 3rd degree.

49.   Know what Gout is.

50.   Know where the meridians begin and end (as there are no pictures on the test).

51.   What muscles make up the rotator cuff? **SITS: supraspinatus, infraspinatus, subscapularis, teres minor**

52.   Types of Contractions; I believe they asked about Isometric.

53.   Questions on Spine curvature; Lordosis, Kyphosis, and scoliosis - know how this affect the muscles in the body and the difference between the curves.

54. Ankle sprains; know the basics and which ligaments get strained from doing what types of movements.

55. What chakra is posterior to the scapula?

    a. chakra 1

    b. chakra 2

    c. chakra 3

    d. chakra 4 (this is the correct answer)

56. What chakra is all energy held in?

    a. sacral

    b. solar plexus

    c. There were two other choices however, the therapist did not remember the other two. Just remember that it is one of the questions asked.

57. What emotion is associated with wood?   **Anger**

58. What endangerment site are you careful of when massaging sartorius? **Femoral artery**

59. What taste is associated with the spleen?   **Sweet**

60. What do you exercise when you have kyphosis?   **Pecs**

61. What vitamin is water soluble? **C**

62. What is accumulation of uric acid?   **Gouty arthritis**

63. What is good for osteoporosis?   **Weight bearing exercises**

64. When running down a hill for a long period of time, what muscle is shortened? **Gastrocnemius**

65. What does cold application do to blood vessels? **Vasoconstriction**

66. Which of the following origin is located under the scapula?

    a.   **teres minor**

    b.   **infraspinatus**

    c.   **subscapularis (correct)**

67.   What muscles are involved in "frozen shoulder" deltoids?

68.   Be sure and know that impetigo is contagious.

69.   What meridian runs parallel to the spine?   **Bladder**

70.   What side of the body is the governing vessel located?   **Posterior**

71.   What is lymphatic drainage good for?
Increase blood flow back to the heart

72.   The skin temperature is regulated by what system?   **Integumentary**

73.   When you find an unconscious person, what is the first thing you should do?
Check the scene

74.   When a client is experiencing anxiety, what is released?
Oxytocin

75.   Why would you not massage on or below the pubic bone?
This is out of scope of practice

76.   What action does the triceps brachii perform?
Extension of elbow, extension of humerus

77.   What aromatherapy is good for respiratory problems?

78.   If you put one hand on back of neck & one hand on sacrum with client lying prone, what is this referred to?   **Energy clearing**

79.   Why would you use sheets on a massage table?

80.   What would you use to clean oily sheets?

81.   The pituitary gland is located behind what bone?   **The sphenoid bone**

82.   If you palpate the Latissimus Dorsi what muscle is deep to it?
The serratus posterior inferior and deep to that, are the erector spinae muscles

83.   You have a 23-year-old female client on your table. You notice she is very thin and is losing hair. You have reason to believe she is anorexic. What do you do?

a. Call her husband

b. Give her psychotherapya

c. Bolster well and proceed with your session cautiously

d. Tell her she needs to go to her doctor, and do not continue with the session

84.   Which muscle is part of the rotator cuff?   **Possible answer: Teres Minor**

85.   What are the muscles of the iliopsoas? **Iliacus and Psoas Major**

86.   What receptors are indicated throwing a baseball?

87.   When the right shoulder is lifted what muscle is activated? **Upper Trapezius**

88.   If after the massage the scapulars are still elevated, what should be stretched? **Possible answer: Rhumboids, upper trapezius**

89.   Gestational Diabetes is mostly at what age? **Over 30 and temporary sometimes during pregnancy**

90.   What is the drug code used to scan medication?   **Possible Answer: UPC**

91.   What is the scope of practice? Some choices were: **moral, ethical, professional.**

92.   What is the antagonist muscle of the piriformis? **Psoas**

93.   Where does the blood pass thru the vena cava? **The superior vena cava returns blood from the upper body to the heart**

94.   What massage helps respiration?

95.   What is locally contraindicated?   **Active herpes**

96.   What weight bearing exercise do you do for orthosclerosis?

97.   What fungus can be spread by a dog? **Ringworm**

98.   What do the external obliques do?

99.   What is it called when the muscle stays tight but is relaxed?   Possible answer: tone abition

100. What is the lateral curve of the spine?   Possible answer: scoliosis

101. Periimysium, Epimysium, and Endomysium cover what? Choices were: bone, tendon, muscle fiber

102. Range of motion is best determined by? Possible answer: Joint Movement Assessments

103. Why must you use light massages on the face?   Possible answer: because of the mandible

104. What is bioenergetics? **The study of the energy transformations in living organisms**

105. What is mixed with essential oils?   **A carrier oil**

106. What type of bath lessons skin nerves? **Carbonated sparkling bath. The human body is enveloped in the carbon dioxide bath, it has an excellent effect on the circulatory system and indirectly it has a calming effect on the whole nervous system.**

107. What is the best form of relaxion for both the client and the therapist?

108. What vitamin is good for the retina and skin? **Vitamin A**

109. What help repair the body?   **Proteins**

110. What muscles causes you eyes to scrench?   **Levator, Frontalis and Mueller Eyelid Muscle**

111. What is in the posterior nerve of the neck? **Phrenic Nerve**

112. What endangered site is contraindicated by the popliteral nerve?

113. What muscle extends the _____and rotates the knee?

114. What process breaks down the food we eat?   **Metabolism**

115.   Elactisity does what to a joint?

116.   What endangered site is on the C1 thru C4?

117.   Blood flow starts to decrease in what phase?   Some choices were: adolesence, toddler, sensence

118.   If abduction the lateral rotators occurs, what muscle is contracted?

119.   If your client has a headache and and you push down on another area, what is it called?

120.   A gift certificate becomes taxable when it is?   Choices were: Expired, Redeemed, Donated

121.   Skin is made up of? **Skin is about 70% water, 25% protein and 2% lipids. The remainder includes trace minerals, nucleic acids, glycosoaminoglycans, proteoglycans and numerous other chemicals.**

122.   Why does scar tissue heal slowly?   Some choices were: no vacisity, no intervention, research for the answer at www.google.com

123.   What is it called when you press an area different from that organ or muscle?
Reflexology

124.   If the scapula is elevated, what muscle is indicated?   Possible answer: traps

125.   What does Universal Precaution do? **Prevents the spread of diseases**

126.   What would be voided if the client came in with the smell of alcohol?
Refuse to keep the appointment

127.   If a client has problem on the medial point of his foot?
Choices were: **drop foot**, over pronation, pigeon toe

128.   Varicose veins are?   **Purple spider like veins, also bue, raised, bulging veins**

129.   Where does urine go after it pass through the bladder? **Urethra**

130.   What does the H in HIV means?   **Human**

131. Protraction does what to the muscle? **Lengthens it**

132. What muscle is attached to the carscoid process? **Biceps brachii**

133. When you are massaging the upper aspect of the pectoral what endanger site must you avoid?   **Subclavian Artery**

134. What do radioulnar joints do? **Rotate**

135. Golgi tendon apparatus inhibits what?   Possible answer: Muscle Contraction

136. What is the origin of the short head of the bicep brachil?   Possible answer: Coracoid process

137. Name a flexor of the hip? Possible answer: Iliopsoas

138. What muscles are involved in the flexor of the humerus?
      Choices are: Pectoralis Major, Anterior Deltoid, Coracobrachailis

139. What flexes the hip and extend the knee?   Possible answer: Quadriceps

140. Palpation is? **Examing the hands, feeling for organ mass, pulse beat, and sense of touch**

141. How do you strech the pectoral muscles?   Possible answer: Abduction and lateral rotation

142. What stroke is defined as a slight trembling of the hand? **Vibration**

143. What is the last part of passage of the colon?
      Choices: Ascending, Descending, Tranverse, **Sigmoid**

144. Where would postural be applied? **In visual assessment.**

145. What would the endangered site be for the popliteal artery? **Femoral artery**

146. Abdominal inhalation requires contraction of what muscle? **the diaphragm**

147. What hydrotherapy modality ls used to decrease pain cellular? **Ice pack**

148.   What muscle is used for forceful inspiration? **external intercostals**

149.   What type of massage should you give on the mandible? **Massage the painful spot with hard, slow, short strokes**

150.   What is Dermatome? This question has two answers. **Dermatome is a surgical instrument and it is also the area of the skin supplied by the nerve root. THIS IS A TRICK QUESTION**

151.   Friction is? **When one layer of tissue is over another, check this out on google.com for other answers**

152.   What technique can assess a weakness in the muscle?

        ROM and Touch for health

153.   What is a frozen shoulder? **A shoulder injury which has four stages: pain, pain and stiffness, stiffness, and resolution.**

154.   The Golgi tendon apparatus measures? **The tension of muscles.**

155.   What oil do you not use by itself? **Essential Oil and sometimes Mineral Oil**

156.   Which micronutrient maintains protoreceptor mechanism of retina and integrity of epithelia? Research for the answer on google.com

1. How much of bleach solution it is used to disinfect?
    - 10%
    - 15%
    - 20%
    - 25%

2. For the IRS, the taxpayers are required to keep records for how many years:
    - 1
    - 3
    - **7 (correct answer)**
    - 10

3. In Chinese medicine, what it is used for effective digestion?
    - Eucalyptus and peppermint
    - **Ginger**
    - **Ginseng and ginkgo Both of these are good for digestion**
    -

4. What is homeostasis?
    - The body at rest
    - **State of balance (correct answer)**

5. In sagittal plane, the ulna is distal to what?
    - wrist
    - olecranon process
    - xiphoid process

6. The elbow hyperextension is not effective because of:
    - olecranon ligaments
    - the muscles that surround the area
    - anterior fluid of elbow
    - posterior bone

7. What type of carbohydrate cannot be digested by the human?
    - **Dietary fiber (cellulose) (correct answer)**
    - Starch from plants
    - Amino acids

8.   Which chakra is associated with communication?
- **Fifth (correct)**
- Fourth
- Second
- First

9.   Which chakra is related to the heart?
- First
- **Fourth (correct)**
- Fifth
- Six

10.   What color chakra is related to the heart?
- **Green (correct)**
- Blue
- Red
- Yellow

11.   What is related to Gallbladder?
- Ears
- Mouth
- Nose
- Eyes

12.   In Chinese medicine what does Middle Burner meridian do?
- Separates and eliminates
- Digestion and nourishment
- Helps body with nutrients

13.   Which tissue helps to connect muscle to bone?
- **Tendon (correct)**
- Ligaments
- Muscle tissue
- Connective tissue

14.   What do ligaments do for the body?
- Connects muscle to muscle
- **Connects bone to bone and binds the joints together**

15.   When assessing a client, the client is asked to do what for the gait test?
- Walk (correct)
- Jump
- Sit
- Stand

16.   When the therapist asses on the client range of motion is called?
- Active (correct)
- Passive

17.   How does the therapist know about the clients past injuries or medical problems?
- **History and interview**
- Observation (I chose this one)
- Range of motion assessment

18.   How heat hydrotherapy helps?
- Reduce cramps (I chose this one)
- Reduce pain
- **Increases blood flow**

19.   A 76 year-old woman who is small-boned and has smoking history. She might be able to develop?
- **Osteoporosis**
- Osteoarthritis

20.   A male client had a foot injury a few months ago, but the foot didn't heal normally. It is hot and red. He might develop?
- Sympathetic dystrophy disease

21.   What causes fascial sheath?
- Myofascial (correct)

22.   What causes lordosis?
- One leg longer than the other
- **Weak Quadratus Lumborum**
- Pubis tilt to side
- Rectus femoris

23. The therapist can help the client with scoliosis by doing what?
    - Compressing the lateral muscle to promote good posture (I chose this one)
    - Aiding the movement of lymphatic fluids towards the nodes

24. What is the first thing the therapist should do with the client having a seizure attack?
    - Put something in their teeth
    - Call emergency services
    - **Hold the client while on the table**
    - Put cushion around the table

25. What part does lordosis affect?
    - **Lumbar (correct)**
    - Thoracic
    - Cervical
    - Sacral

26. Why does cartilage take a long time to heal?
    - Poorly blood flow (a possible answer) but research this for sure

27. How can a therapist help a client with Rheumatoid arthritis?
    - Range of motion
    - Circulate the synovial fluids (possible answer)

28. What is Torticollis?
    - Erect spine
    - **Wryneck (correct)**

29. How lordosis is described in the body?
    - Referred pain
    - Neuralgia
    - Chronic fatigue syndrome

30. What is a failure of the vertebral arch?
    - Huntington's disease
    - **Spina bifida** Parkinson's disease
    - Epilepsy

31.   What are the first symptoms of osteoarthritis?

-
-

32.   Where is goiter located?

- **Thyroid gland**
- Thalamus
- Pancreas

33.   What symptoms are associated with wheezing, coughing?

- Asthma
- **Bronchitis**

34.   Anemia is cause by lacking of?

- **Vitamin B12 and iron**
-

35.   What nutrient helps with the formation of teeth, bones?

- Vitamin C
- Calcium
- **Vitamin D**

36.   What should a therapist do if a client comes with the influence of alcohol?

- **Reschedule**
- Proceed with massage
- Offer the client a cup of coffee

37.   Myocardial infarction refers to?

- **Heart attack**
- Stroke
- Hodgkin's disease

38.   What infection is contagious from person to person contact?

- Hives
- Acne
- Psoriasis
- **Herpes**

39.   What thick muscle is hard to palpatate in the triangle of the neck?

- **Sternocleidomastoid**
- Axillary

40.   What part of the body can have effect by applying hydrotherapy and scent oil?

- **Superficial integument**

41.   What tendon is cause by tendonitis?

- **Golgi tendon organ**

42.   In oriental medicine, what two organs are related to Earth element?

- **Stomach and spleen**
- Bladder and kidney
- Lung and large intestine

43.   The stomach meridian is located where:

- Lateral aspect of the chest, passes up the anterolateral, the arm to the root of the thumbnail
- **Run over the face, passes down the throat, end at the root of the second toenail**
- Begins on thorax, runs up the arm, ends middle finger

44.   When promoting reflexology, the therapist can identify problem because:

- **Tightness in some parts of the feet (correct)**
- Part of the feet turn red

45.   What type of movement is related with moving the body from its longitudinal position?

- Extension
- Flexion
- Rotation
- Circumduction

46.   What type of modality penetrates deep tissue muscle?

- Therapeutic touch
- Trager
- **Shiatsu**
- Polarity

47.   Which hormone is related to the sympathetic nervous system?

- **corticotropin-releasing hormone**
- Insulin
- Oxytocin

48.   It is contraindicated to do?
- **Heavy precaution below the thoracic region**
- Heavy precaution on the extremities

49.   Which is the largest organ?
- **Skin**

50.   Which muscle relaxes when inhalation is involved?
- External oblique
- Internal Intercostal
- Internal oblique
- **Diaphragm**

51. Which organ is affected in a long term disease?
- Ulcer
- **Liver**
- Gallbladder

52.   What type of technique is adequate to perform for the fascial adheretions?
- Friction)
- Deep tissue
- Effleurage
- Gliding strokes -   research for the correct answer

53.   The muscle contracts and shortness during contraction; the same force of contraction is maintained throughout the movement (Also, this question was written in the way that agonist and antagonist do the movement of contraction):
- **Isotonic**
- Isometric
- Eccentric
- Synergist

54.   Which of the following is a correct lift posture?
- Facing the lift
- Knee flex touching together
- Rotate stand (possible answer)

55. Physiologic effects of massage are beneficial:
    - **Increases flexibility and cellular metabolism**

56. Massage effects in muscular system:
    - **Reduces muscle pain and cramps**

57. What type of movement should be applied for shoulder pain?
    - Kneading (possible answer)
    - Gliding
    - Friction

58. The purpose of stretching:
    - **Improve mobility and flexibility)**

59. By providing first aid, how many breaths per minute does an adult needs?
    - 12-18 (possible answer)
    - 1-10

60. What is the first aid for skeletal muscles?
    - **Rest, ice, compression and elevation**

61. In Chinese medicine, acupressure is fulfilled when the body is?
    - Full
    - Empty
    - **Balanced**

63. Yoga is effective to practice because:
    - **Exercises mentally and emotional control of the body**

64. What are moral principles?
    - **ethics**

65. The massage practitioner/bodyworker is known by the client in "role (dual) relationship":
    - gives what it makes the client happy
    - knows the client from a non-therapeutic place (possible answer)
    - discusses other clients problems with the clients
    - warms and stimulates the client

66. The practitioner/bodyworker is violating the code of ethics by:
   - **asking the client on a date**
   - protect client's privacy

67. Income that is equal to the income earned minus the revenue (worded something like this):
   - gross income
   - **net income**